A Theological Journey

Christian Faith and Human Salvation

Ghislain Lafont, O.S.B.

Translated by John J. Burkhard, O.F.M. Conv.

A Michael Glazier Book

LITURGICAL PRESS
Collegeville, Minnesota

www.litpress.org

A Michael Glazier Book published by Liturgical Press

Originally published as *Promenade en théologie* © Lethielleux, un département de Méta-Editions, Paris, 2003.

Cover design by Ann Blattner. Illustration: *Tower 1*, 1923–26, Lyonel Feininger. Kunstmuseum, Basel, Switzerland.

1   2   3   4   5   6   7   8

Library of Congress Cataloging-in-Publication Data

Lafont, Ghislain.
    [Promenade en theologie. English]
    A theological journey : christian faith and human salvation / Ghislain Lafont.
        p.   cm.
    "A Michael Glazier Book."
    Includes bibliographical references and index.
    ISBN-13: 978-0-8146-5213-8
    1. Theology—History.   2. Church history.   I. Title.
BT75.3.L3413 2007
230'.2—dc22   2007012314

CONTENTS

Preface

There are times when a theologian of a certain age is invited to write a short, synthetic initiation, somewhat simplified and more readable than what he has written to date. The theologian might choose to leave aside weighty research methods demanded by a more academic style of writing, in order to recapture for a moment what he has formerly or recently developed at great length. Some of the great theologians of the past have left us wonderful examples of such writing. I think of the *Catechetical Orations* of St. Gregory of Nyssa (ca. 330–395), or the *Breviloquium* of St. Bonaventure (1221–1274), or the *Compendium theologiae* of St. Thomas Aquinas (1225–1274). Each of these works has become a classic. In our days, the great Catholic theologian of the twentieth century, Karl Rahner, S.J. (1904–1984), toward the end of his life wanted to present a book that summarized and ordered the many insights he had garnered. He wanted to speak about the Christian faith in all the domains of theology and culture he had addressed in the course of his years of study, writing, teaching, and lecturing. This was to become his masterpiece, *Foundations of Christian Faith* (1976). In French, one can point to Louis Bouyer's *Christian Initiation* (1960) and to Bernard Sesboüé's recent *Croire* (1999).

I do not pretend to be the equal of these masters, but I have still taken the risk of writing my own short summary. I call it a "journey," first because the word simply and directly expresses my desire to show the reader the right paths to take. "Journey" also signifies that today one cannot pretend to introduce someone to theology without making a short road trip through its history. As we realize better today, time is not extrinsic to reflection but partly constitutive of it. We have to "take a trip" if we are going to understand, always with the presumption that in space as varied as Christian thought is, many trips are possible. I invite you to the one I've written, though there are others. Finally, a "journey" should lead us somewhere. That is why the itinerary proposed in this book opens out on a more synthetic treatment of Christian faith. There is reciprocity between the route taken and the exposition of the faith. This is an aspect of the way of learning or knowing called today the "hermeneutical circle." The paths of the journey are more or less clearly marked off because the traveler presses on toward the goal of the trip. But the terminus cannot be appreciated for what it is if the reader refuses to walk the route chosen.

PART ONE

INTRODUCTION
The Road Traveled

FROM SALVATION TO REFLECTION

Toward the end of his life, the German philosopher and agnostic Martin Heidegger (1889–1976), was so perplexed by the floundering situation of Western civilization, that he let slip a phrase that has often been repeated, "Only a god could save us." One is reminded of the similarity of his formula to that which St. Paul read on an inscription on an altar in the Areopagus of Athens, "To an unknown god" (Acts 17:23). At the time, the Athenians were passing through a period of profound uncertainty, and the apparent *Pax Romana* of an empire built on world domination could only paper it over.

To be saved. What does that mean? Surely, it must mean that one is launched on a path that enables one to escape all-encircling evil, without being transported immediately to another world but by receiving life-giving powers that bestow progressive and assured healing of injuries inflicted, purification from collusion with evil, and the possibility of being reconciled with oneself, with others, and eventually with "god."[1]

---

[1] The use of the lower case for *god* indicates that we are not talking about a personal God, clearly distinct from human beings and from the world, while at the same time having a relationship with them, as is the case of the God of Judeo-Christian revelation.

1

Put positively, to be saved would signify receiving revelation of "meaning," something that transcends the feeling of being "lost" in a quagmire of absurd suffering. One would be able to lead what the ancients called the "good life" in spite of inevitable hardships, or more simply put, to know "happiness." Or again, to be saved is to be convinced that one is on the path that leads to the fulfillment of essential human desires that come to expression in the cultural and religious symbols (see glossary) of humanity as a whole. In this regard, "ultimate meaning" would be the accomplishment and the culmination of history. However, there would have to be meaning in the present as well, since every situation is capable of being lived or transformed as love of "god" and of human beings, and as growth in the knowledge of the truth.

To be saved. The word salvation also signifies that healing and the happy life are beyond our grasp, so great is the gulf between what we humans experience and what we aspire to. This fact explains why Heidegger and the Athenians could express the hidden conviction, "Only a god could save us." But which god? The gods known to the Greek pantheon could not save. Proof of this fact is found in the experience that one was always unhappy. And if philosophy called the immanent forces that mysteriously traversed history "gods," experience once again demonstrated that they could not save. In the end, there was only the "unknown god."

Saint Paul claimed to reveal the identity of this "unknown god" to the Athenian devotees. Yes, only a god can save us, and this is God's name: the God who raised Jesus Christ from the dead. Christianity has never deviated from this precise identification of God. Today, the same as yesterday, the Christian awaits a salvation that is defined in terms of faith in God, of course, but a God who is revealed in Jesus of Nazareth, a specific person who lived in the Middle East at the beginning of the Common Era. He was an Israelite, who expressed his life and his teaching in the particular religious way of his people, all the while proposing a renewed and open interpretation of that way. Like many prophets before him, he was rejected and killed. Then, some of his disciples began immediately to testify that after he had died they saw him alive and spoke with him. This was the experience they laid claim to when they proclaimed that "God has raised Jesus from the dead" (Acts 3:15). Just such a resurrection, for that is what these Christian communities believed, gave ultimate meaning to their existence, that of humanity and of the cosmos. It was a matter of a step toward a state of perfect communion with God, with Jesus as guide and goal. In this way, the resurrection distinctly confirmed the life, the example, and the teaching of Jesus, and the resurrection also illuminated the way in this world by robbing death of its power. Moreover, by meditating on the words and deeds of Jesus during his lifetime, both in their own terms and in light of the Jewish Scriptures, the disciples came to the conviction that Jesus was not only God's final envoy to men and women, not only the Messiah, the Christ,[2] but that he enjoyed a unique closeness to God, an insight which came to expression in the title they gave him—"Son of God."

Christianity was and is what we would call a "movement." It gathers together "those who look to Jesus in faith as the author of salvation and the principle of unity and peace"[3] and who found their lives on the Gospel of Jesus Christ. Not only do they believe in Jesus Christ, but they also confess that Christ has sent a Spirit of holiness who is invisibly present in the world and who inspires them in their personal and collective conduct. Christians also believe that their fundamental religious rites lead them to Christ, unite them with one another, and lead them to God. Together they await the end-time,[4] a moment that signifies all of humanity's entry into permanent and definitive communion with God. This "movement" has a name, "church," that is, the people that has been called forth and called together by Christ.

Under these conditions, Christians have always been set on witnessing to their faith and announcing Jesus Christ to others, so that they, too, might "join the movement," live a life of happiness, and finally be saved. The question might be posed: if Christianity is all about witnessing to salvation given by God in Jesus Christ, where is there place for "theology" or "Christian reflection"? In point of fact, from the very moment that Jesus disappeared from human view, it was necessary to find the right words to speak about him. It was also necessary to render an account

---

[2] Jesus' title of "Christ" is the root of the word for the movement that came to be known as *Christianity*.

[3] The Dogmatic Constitution on the Church (*Lumen Gentium*), no. 9. Norman P. Tanner, ed., *Decrees of the Ecumenical Councils,* vol. 2 (Washington, D.C.: Georgetown University Press, 1990), p. 856.

[4] This is the translation I have preferred throughout the book for the events associated with the return of Jesus in glory or the parousia, the event that the early Christians awaited with hope and that they thought was imminent. Other translations that one finds are "the end times," "the end of time," "the last things," "the eschaton," and "the end of the world." See the explanation in the "A Glossary of Terms" [translator].

of this testimony, that is, to show whether this mysterious person, Jesus Christ, could respond to the infinitely varied expectations of people in time, especially as the ages have grown farther and farther distant from the earthly life of Jesus. How, too, can Jesus Christ respond to men and women across the space determined by race, nationality, culture, and history that give each human group its own particular imprint? The missionary task of announcing Jesus Christ has not been without its efficacy either. Wherever it has taken root, Christianity has contributed to the modification of human cultures and the systems of thought by which human beings have attempted to give meaning to their lives and to history, as we shall see shortly. For its part, Christian reflection on the gospel (see glossary) has received much from the encounter with other cultures, to the extent that Christianity's recourse to certain words, patterns of thought, and various practices has permitted it to advance in its perception of God, of the world, of what it is to be human, and of Jesus Christ himself—all as more precisely situated in human terms.

Such a process of reciprocal influence is endless. New experiences, new mind-sets, and new words, when applied to the Christian mystery (see glossary) in different contexts, provoke yet other expressions. It follows, then, that if Jesus himself has come to his final fulfillment, by reason of his resurrection, and if he lives in perfect communion with God and the Spirit, the words that we use here below to speak of him are truly "infinite." It is in this sense that Christianity, understood as faith and salvation, becomes reflection. Nonetheless, such reflection needs to take care that it remains within the revealed boundaries of salvation itself. If it fails to do this, it becomes yet another form of wisdom or philosophy.

In reality, Christianity as theology is not a singular reflection but reflections, in the plural. This is true because in time cultures evolve, and so the ideas that drive them are changed. The same can be said of the differences that result in space. Even when we can point to a specific place, the propositions that try to enunciate the meaning of faith can emerge from sensibilities and understandings that are quite diverse. "Christian reflection" is constituted by plurality (see glossary) and by the contemplation of more or less irreconcilable differences. On the one hand, plurality can be seen as an advantage, whereas irreconcilable differences are a disadvantage, or at the least a difficulty, for the faith. Now is probably the moment for the reader to note that the presentation in this little book is inspired by Latin Catholicism, which is to say that it is far from exhausting all possible perspectives on Christian thought. In any case, it should be evident from the start that the various forms of

Christian reflection have no final meaning except to the extent that they are intimately connected to faith in Jesus Christ and to the conduct that results from a faith in search of the salvation it hopes for so longingly. We might further remark that Christian reflection follows the law of all authentic thought: true philosophies arise from the love of wisdom because it is the very source of salvation. They enable reason, but in view of a response that addresses the whole human being.

OUR PROPOSED ITINERARY

In this first part, we will attempt to retrace the great stages of Christian reflection. These stages need to be considered in relation to the cultural changes that have occurred, against which Christianity had to be situated, while always maintaining the originality of the ideas and the practices as they presented themselves to it. Thus, speaking comprehensively, Western culture is the result of a never-ending process of at times polemical, at other times peaceful, confrontations between various humanisms and revelation. We will observe first of all that the earliest treatises possess special value for two reasons. First, their proximity to the person, life, and message of Jesus Christ endows them with special privilege; and second, Christians recognize in these writings a value that is almost transcendent because they believe their Scripture to be inspired by God (chapter 1). In order to simplify the presentation, we will claim that Christian reflection is formed in the course of time by confrontation with three challenges issued one after the other. The first is the confrontation with "religion," or in other words, with cult and mysticism. This is how one can approach ancient theology (chapter 2). The second is the confrontation with "wisdom," or in other terms, with humanism. We have in mind here the medieval period (chapter 3). The third is the confrontation with "motion," or in other words with history and its infinite development. These confrontations are the theological efforts that give pride of place gradually to historical change in Christian reflection, even to the point of giving it the principal place. This movement can be seen from the Enlightenment up to our own day (chapter 4).

On the other hand, one might consider the general inspiration of these confrontations, and then we can reduce the three currents to two. "Classical" theologies develop in a world marked by the idea of stability (chapters 2 and 3). The earth is fixed, the rhythms of life recur again and again, and the revolutions of the stars in the sky are regular and circular. Order and harmony appear to be supreme values and are the signs of the divine. It is only a matter of elaborating Christian reflection in terms of these values and of rejecting everything opposed to them, which would be error and the perversion of thought. These early thinkers did not have the means necessary to reason positively about what is characteristic of the phenomena of rupture and the unexpected. They were captive to reflection that is governed by *space*. On the other hand, "modern" theologies rightly attempt to address the issues that classical theologies were not capable of addressing (chapter 4). They privilege those elements of Christianity that arise from the unpredictable nature of freedom, as well as from the direction history is taking and from its inherent tragedy. Here, one is attracted to reflection that is intent on interpreting *time*.

If we wanted to speak in chronological terms, we might say that the ancient theologies extend throughout the first millennium of Christian thought, from St. Irenaeus of Lyons (ca. 115–202) and Origen (ca. 185–254) to St. Bonaventure (1221–1274) and St. Thomas Aquinas (1225–1274). Modern theologians, then, would stretch over the six centuries that separate the death of the last two-named great doctors to the accession of Pope Leo XIII (1878–1903). Our hypothesis is that these two great orientations, if they cannot be completely harmonized, are still not opposed to one another. "Truth" and "History" do not admit a third term that is capable of containing both of them. Still, one does not have to choose one to the exclusion of the other, but one must try as far as possible to find a kind of dialectical interplay where they manifest themselves by turns and are enriched by the confrontation. Scripture includes the Law, the Prophets, and Wisdom, whereas Western philosophy is built on the twofold and contrary foundations of Parmenides' *Absolute* (fifth century B.C.E.) and Heraclitus' *flux* (sixth–fifth century B.C.E.). Neither pole can be reduced to the other, but the thinker must constantly navigate between both. As for contemporary theology, we are unquestionably too close to it to judge its success. We are still in the midst of a movement that began in the middle of the nineteenth century. Have we not been about practicing this very dialectic between history and truth since Friedrich Nietzsche (1844–1900) and Sigmund Freud (1856–1939), Adolf von Harnack (1851–1930) and Julius Wellhausen (1844–1918), Maurice Blondel (1861–1949), and Père Marie-Joseph Lagrange, O.P. (1855–1938) up to the theologians known to us today, who come after the founding of the World Council of Churches (1948) and the Second Vatican Council (1962–1965)? That is what we must consider later on.

Chapter One

THE SCRIPTURES

SCRIPTURAL PRINCIPLES

If we approach theology chronologically, we note that three elements inspired the first reflections on Jesus. First of all, the recollection of Jesus' words, deeds, and actions was preserved in the disciples' memory, then communicated orally to whoever chose to listen to them, and finally written down in a variety of forms which constitute what today we call the New Testament—the synthesis and the collection of the oral and written tradition relating to Jesus. Second, we find the Jewish Scriptures (usually called the Old Testament), which formed the base of Jesus' own message and how he interpreted himself and his mission. New Testament authors never tired of searching the Scriptures for anticipations of Jesus and for keys to understanding his life, death, and resurrection. They accomplished this task of correlating Jesus to the Old Testament by employing the usual methods of interpreting the Scripture that the sages and scribes of Israel themselves had used. Finally, to the extent that it applied, in most cases the New Testament authors addressed Gentiles or wrote to them, first of all by using their own language, Greek, and not the Aramaic spoken in Palestine and by Jesus himself. In this way, they drew on a common fund of Hellenistic wisdom and expressions that also left their mark on the earliest Christian interpretations of the facts.

AWAITING CHRIST

For the first generations of Christians, Jesus was someone who was expected to return to his people and who would bring Israel's history to its conclusion. But Jesus would also bring the history of all people to its fulfillment. In Jesus and with him, all of humanity would be transformed and established forever in a relationship of happiness with God. Christians employed a host of poetic expressions to state their convictions. They spoke of a "banquet" and of a "wedding feast," and even of a "kingdom" (see glossary). Above all else, Jesus is the one who would bring about the millennial aspiration of humanity for union with God, the millennial aspiration of the Jews for the perfect covenant with God.

Jesus arrived on the scene just at the moment when what might be called "the question of God" reached a decisive turn. The religious history of Israel had experienced the ups and downs of a constant struggle with idolatry. In order to resist the misery that often came in the wake of phenomena like famine, drought, and inevitable death, or in order to be victorious in their unending combat with their hostile neighbors, the Israelites, like the other populations, were tempted to address prayers and offer sacrifices to unknown gods—forces of nature and protectors of the people who were dedicated to them. The whole of the Law and the teaching of the prophets, in historical conditions that varied greatly, were directed toward demonstrating to Israel that its God was unique and that he entered into a covenant with them as his people. They were challenged to put their confidence in him, to accept him as their stronghold and their refuge. If they did so, and despite all appearances to the contrary, they could rest assured that God would give them prosperity and success. Eventually, a "history of God" took hold of the heart of the people, or at least of the hearts of the most lucid among them. There emerged the perception that God was stronger than all the gods of their neighboring peoples, and stronger than the gods of the strongest nations, even if they were victorious temporarily. In time, the Israelites confessed that God was unique, a God who reigns as a sovereign over the whole earth, that the other "gods" were nothing but pretenses, idols fashioned by human hands and devoid of all power. These "gods" possessed no reality and were empty shams. Finally, they claimed that God was not only the ruler of the world and the vicissitudes of history, but that their God was the wise creator of the universe.

However powerless the Israelites felt in the face of the constantly succeeding empires in the East—one more powerful than the preceding, with Rome as the final empire—Israel came to the conclusion that she was the witness of this unique God, the creator of the world and the solicitous friend of humanity. The Israelites remained true to this faith and they awaited a political restoration that would permit them to visibly express God's kingship, over Jerusalem first of all, and then by their agency, over all humanity. In this way, little by little, there emerged the figure of a "servant of God," the last of the prophets, who would come at the end to establish God's kingly rule.

In Jesus' day, the fidelity of the people expressed itself through great respect for the Law of Moses, a sign of God's election and covenant. Nevertheless, the respect shown the Law varied from place to place and from group to group. Some Jews centered their observance in a more personal way on moral and spiritual actions that included the founding rites of circumcision and observing the Sabbath. These Jews kept their distance from other Jews whose piety was more directed to the public cult of the temple. In either case, confessing the uniqueness of God and the exalted status of the Law remained the two pillars of Jewish faith and hope.

For his part, Jesus can also be located within the perspective of his people, but he added the nuances of deeper interiority and a greater sense of being in relationship to the Law's observance and to cultic practice. Rites are good, of course, but their celebration needs to be brought closer to a connection with the concrete needs of persons, especially the poor. The commandments are holy, of course, but the Israelite is called to interiorize them and to understand them in the light of the first commandment, and the second which is similar to it—love is the very heart and the driving force of the Law. Jesus stressed God's proximity to human beings. In this way, he highlighted the aspects of tenderness and mercy developed by the prophets before him, and Jesus' habit of calling God "Father" reinforced his message. At the same time, Jesus' representation of God stressed the fact that purely exterior observance of the Law is wholly unsatisfactory if it is not animated by love. It goes without saying, then, that Jesus' message, one that is completely traditional within Judaism and yet genuinely new, throughout his ministry would raise the question as to his identity. Was he a prophet? Was he Elias who was to return? Was he John the Baptist risen from the dead? (See Mark 6:14-15.)

Following the resurrection, there is little doubt that the first Judeo-Christian community, with James, the "brother" of Jesus, and Peter, the chosen disciple, as its leaders, would interpret this powerful divine intervention as the confirmation of Jesus' message. Christ's exaltation confirms what he taught. The final identity of God is spelled out as the Father and Jesus as the Messiah sent by God to gather in the dispersed people of Israel. And as regards the obedience due to God, it is an interior observance of the Law as preached by the Master, coupled with a flexibility regarding rites and practices that does not diminish but rather heightens their value in the eyes of God. Faith in Christ distinguishes his community from other spiritual movements in Judaism, but it does not isolate his community from them.

Saint Paul

Then Paul arrives on the scene. He was a Jewish Pharisee, in other words, a man committed to fidelity to the Law of Moses and to the traditions maintained by his people. He was convinced that only strict observance of the Law would prepare for the kingly rule of God. He commenced by violently opposing the "Christian way," that is to say, the specific interpretation that Jesus had given to the observance of the Law and that promoted a mixed community of Jews and Christians. At the start, Paul refused this new teaching about God, just as he rejected the identity of Jesus as the Messiah. Then all of a sudden, following his abrupt conversion, Paul dedicated himself immediately and without warning to preaching the Christian message, doing so with the same passion he had shown formerly when he persecuted the Christians he condemned. Now he affirmed that faith in Christ, as well as accepting his teaching and his practices, is the sole source of salvation, for both Jews and pagans. In a move that can only be characterized as a love/hate relationship with his Jewish roots, Paul tried to show the absolute superiority of faith in Christ as compared with the rigorous Jewish observance of the Law that he had earlier defended. But what he does not reject is the mission of the chosen people and his membership, past and present, in that people. This preoccupation led Paul to continue to expand his resolve and to situate himself in the perspective of a global vision of the history of human beings. Let us try to sketch the outlines of Paul's interpretation.

The definitive establishment of God's kingly rule, which was the hope-filled expectation by Jews to which Paul remained committed, supposes the radical healing of all the world's evils. In the tradition of Israel, which Jesus did not repudiate, evil is bound up with the origins of sin. In other words, evil is bound up with the culpable ignorance of human beings, themselves incapable of understanding their true calling, handed over to passions that render them idolatrous with respect to God, and that turns them into enemies of one another. Death is the sign of sin and indicates total failure. In consequence, before God's kingly rule can be established, there must first be a reconciliation. This exigency explains why Paul pursues a meditation on the way Christ effected reconciliation for us with God and with each other. The dreadful death of a condemned and crucified Jesus is the means by which sins are forgiven. Jesus' death is interpreted in terms of sacrifice and redemption. Paul lived in a culture, whether Jewish or pagan, for which sacrifice, or the offering of a victim to obtain reconciliation and reestablish communion, was something taken for granted and assumed by all. Paul had no difficulty in taking up this and other related notions, in order to express the meaning of Jesus' death. But Paul claimed that the love of God who hands his Son over for our reconciliation and the love of Christ who offers himself, was the heart of this sacrifice and gave it its meaning. This was true as well for the Son, who also pursued the same goal of reconciliation through love. Jesus passed through death, the sign of sin, that is, the sign of our human estrangement from God and from each other. His resurrection vanquished death and so posed the first stone of a transformed world. His return in glory would mark the transformed world's fulfillment.

Paul drew from this vision of salvation a consequence of capital importance, one that would place him in a delicate relationship to the Judeo-Christian community of Jerusalem, from the beginning of his ministry right up to the end. In Paul's eyes, faith in Jesus Christ "who was handed over for our transgressions and was raised for our justification" (Rom 4:25) is the sole approach that permits us, Jews and pagans alike, to receive salvation from God. Judaism's founding rite of circumcision and the practices found in the traditional commentaries on the Law must give way to a faith that welcomes justification coming to us as divine gift. Paul does not deny that such rites and observances retain a certain pedagogical value for Jewish-Christian converts, but they are not necessary for the salvation of all. They are of no concern to Christians who have converted from paganism and they do not define what it is to be a Christian. The only law that perdures, once one has been saved by faith, is the law of love, which is summed up in respect for one's neighbor and is incumbent on all Christians, Jews and Gentiles alike.

With the help of this fundamental outline of Christian faith, Paul continues his reflection on Christ and pursues the reality and the manifestation of Jesus as it were to its roots, while he awaits at the end of history the full revelation of the faith. Holy Scripture speaks of Adam, the first human being created by God. In fact, according to Paul, Christ is the true Adam, the one by whom the adventure began on the earliest days of creation, in accordance with God's original plan, and who gives creation its meaning (see 1 Cor 15:45-49). In a variety of ways, Paul develops a vision of history in which humanity is divided into two groups of human beings. The first is the Jewish people who had their origins with Abraham and who have benefited from a special revelation and from a unique covenant with God, but who were unfaithful. The second is the rest of humanity, the Gentiles, who in spite of the light of conscience, strayed into the shadows of enmity with God. God's plan as it were rises above the division and surmounts this twofold trespass (see Gal 3:6-14). From the beginning, God predestined Christ to effect a reconciliation of these two peoples with him and to fashion from both a single body with Christ as the head. The key to the whole of history is Christ, who not only was thought and willed before he even appeared, but who, in a way that Paul does not render more precise for us, even preexisted everything that came to be. The end-time will come when Christ, the true Adam in whom history has reached its definitive meaning, will come and hand over a reunited and reconciled humanity to God.

THE SYNOPTIC GOSPELS

The Christian Scriptures composed after the letters of St. Paul were narratives that are called "gospels." Each gospel has its own distinctive character that is due to the personal genius of the writer, his reason for writing it, and his attention to the needs of the community in which he lived or for which he was writing. Still, its peculiar quality did not mean that each gospel was absolutely original and did not have anything in common with the other gospels. Each one is based on recollections of the person of Jesus and of his actions and teachings that each community retained. Observances that Jesus drew from Jewish tradition and that were eventually changed in form and significance can also be found in the gospels. Finally, the gospels include interpretations of these data that are the products of prophets who belonged to the earliest Christian communities. All of these factors were organized in service of the cross and resurrection of Jesus. These two events, which were really unexpected and accessible only to faith, clarify with a light both obscure and radiant at the same time all that Jesus said and did. The cross and resurrection alone permit one to really confess the true identity of the Lord and to discern what the subsequent life of Christians was like.

From this point of view, one can discern the outline of the Gospel's presentation of Jesus as it emerged historically. First of all, it was a teaching that centered on the coming of the kingly rule of God, whose qualities of interiority and truth we have already considered. Jesus' preaching, which was backed up by his miracles, demanded a conversion that was both personal and ordered to the people of God. It would appear that Jesus elicited some real but fickle enthusiasm among the people. Still, he did attract a strong following among a handful of disciples who were probably no more insightful about his identity than the crowds were, but who were deeply attracted to him personally. Jesus' teaching and religious observance, and the messianic identity they hinted at, increasingly encountered strong opposition from certain quarters of his Jewish contemporaries. These included men whose purity of life demanded the strict interpretation and observance of the Law and the tradition of the ancients, as well as the temple priests who were charged with the performance of the liturgy. Persecution and death appeared to Jesus, and eventually to his disciples also, as the unavoidable way for God's kingly rule to be initiated. The way one goes about obeying the commandments necessarily contains an aspect of crucifixion that will always be how a disciple of Christ follows him. Finally, Jesus' death and resurrection disclosed a deeper dimension of their reality: in a mysterious way, God's own true visage is revealed in the face of the crucified Jesus. In Mark's Gospel, for example, throughout his life Jesus rejects any characterizations that smack of something glorious in his person, something exalted about him. Jesus might have seen this danger in his miracles, or in such titles as "Messiah" and "Son of God." Titles like these do not mean that Jesus did not understand himself in such terms, but they could not express something essential about him. Only Jesus' death on the cross could reveal the profound depths of his divine sonship. The quality of self-giving manifested by the cross discloses to everyone of good will something about who God is. At the moment of Jesus' death, the pagan centurion at the cross confesses as much: "Truly this man was the Son of God" (Mark 15:39). Ever since, the church has not ceased to meditate on the relationship between divine glory and the cross. The cross qualifies both who Jesus is and how the Christian should live.

Saint John

It is well known that among the gospels, the Gospel of John has its own form and is unique. Together with his brother James and Peter, another disciple, John was a witness to a number of moments of glory and sorrow in Jesus' life. A complex ensemble of writings consisting of various literary genres has been attributed to him, and it is entirely possible that some of these writings can be traced directly to John. The Johannine writings consider Jesus more from the point of view of God who, from the very beginning, has communicated Godself to creation, than from the point of view of our universal human need for salvation. To accomplish this, John employs themes that were developed in the Old Testament: the prophetic word of God spoken to men and women; wisdom which is in God's presence and sent to creation; and the Son, both divine and human. John develops these themes in a way that highlights the very center of the mystery: "The Word became flesh / and made his dwelling among us" (John 1:14), a foundational verse that gave rise to a term characteristic of Christianity—Incarnation. God had always been understood as speaking with humanity, and especially with the people of Israel, but with Jesus his word became flesh, his wisdom fashioned humanity, his glory became manifest, his fatherhood became concrete. This did not mean that the details of Jesus' life were unimportant, however. On the contrary, Jesus' life is understood as manifesting God's glory and inviting humanity to penetrate it. From Christ's fullness, we have all received. If humanity, in faith and love, welcomes God's revelation in the incarnate Word, humans in turn can become children of God and enter into a relationship of truth and love with God that is the very heart of salvation. To know God is salvation, or in Johannine language, to know God is eternal life.

Whether we look to Jesus' life and teaching, or judge his destiny in the context of a universal history of humanity, or meditate on his person from the point of view of the mystery of total communication of the divine to us, Christ alone is the savior. Christ alone is the one by whom everyone, Jew and Gentile, receives purification and redress from the evil that has taken hold of the world. Christ alone is the revelation and the knowledge of God that manifests and transfigures the ultimate meaning of human existence.

CONCLUSION

To sum up, we can say that the Scriptures, in a way that is both infinitely varied and yet forms a unity, express three inseparable poles: faith in Jesus Christ, Lord and savior; confession of God as one, Father of Jesus and Father of all humanity; and the observance of a law of life that is summed up in the twofold commandment of love. These three poles are animated by the grace of the Holy Spirit sent by God and are found in a delicate balance of continuity and change with regard to the revelation which God alone has worked throughout Israel's history, in the many literary texts and historical forms it has taken in time. They can be considered the reference points we need in order to understand the development of the understanding of faith—which is not yet finished, by the way—in the long course of the centuries of God's dealings with humanity.

Chapter Two

THE PERIOD OF THE "FATHERS" AND OF THE "COUNCILS"
Spiritual Worship and Mystical Theology

THE ENCOUNTER WITH HELLENISTIC CULTURE

From the very earliest generations of Christians, the Christian message spread throughout the Roman world and had to confront the Hellenistic culture that constituted the world of those who converted to Christianity and the social context of the local churches that were founded. The most profound characteristic of this culture, and the one that marked early Christians, was the search for *union* and *unity* that was at the very center of the idea of the divine, of finitude, of the world, of knowledge, and of evil. The wise man or woman in the Hellenistic world was convinced that ultimate happiness was found in a mysterious relationship with a god who paradoxically cannot be known. In the schools of thought of the day, this god is completely immanent in the world as the force, or as the reason, keeping it in existence. Conversely, this god is totally beyond all that exists and is characterized by words that do not so much express clearly as suggest his reality, words like Being, Light, Silence, Goodness, and Truth, among others. The wise man or woman is in search of the path that will lead to being joined with this god, that he or she perhaps comes from, and will result ultimately in being "one" with him. But the wise must take into account the helplessness of the situation they find themselves in at the moment, and that means specifically that they must ponder "evil," that is, everything that holds them in estrangement from this god and keeps them in bondage to the limitations of their being and their spirit. It is not easy to come to terms with such evil, because if god is beyond human knowledge, it is difficult to know what pleases or displeases him. To such a one, the world appears shot through with pain and disasters that afflict the person with the sense of being both their victim and of being responsible for them. In this situation, nothing is very clear and everything is threatening. The only escape from this widespread sense of culpability is to lose oneself in god.

Without making too much of the differences of opinions on these matters, we can say that in general access to ultimate "knowledge" took place through cult and mysticism. By cult, I mean an ensemble of symbolically performed acts, often quite cruel, and ethical actions and techniques that render the human being favorable, not to the unknown god who remains distant and hardly interested in such gestures, but to the world of spirits and lesser gods who inhabit the space that separates earth and heaven. These spirits govern the natural phenomena so essential for human life. Ultimately, they rule over life and death and can either facilitate or impede the path to god. By mysticism, on the other hand, the wise, who are conscious of the impotence of cult but are still desirous of union with the unknown god, traverse the depths of the spirit and reach the recesses of the heart where it is possible in silence to meet the ultimate divinity and to attain "knowledge."[1]

Christianity, also being keenly interested in the question of the relation of the human being with the divine and with the meaning of human existence, found it easy to draw on these perspectives of the Hellenistic world which seemed to be consistent with the language and thought forms of the Gospel of John in particular. As such, Christianity in this period gave

---

[1] In order to understand better the environment of the pagan world at the time of the fathers of the church, we need only pay close attention to certain aspects of our own world. Our contemporaries do not so much know "cult" in the proper sense of the word but a variety of substitutes for it. Examples are found in the popularity of astrology or in the preferences we have or the mass gatherings we form, things that are not really religious, but which assuage our spiritual insecurity. Thus, we speak of "cult films" or of the "High Masses of our sports stadiums." At the level of mysticism today, people surrender themselves both in theory and by acts of generosity to the various wisdoms of the East that are thought to lead them to "knowledge."

privileged place to oneness with the divine, and the sense of being whole in oneself. Nonetheless, the Bible insisted on certain decisive points in the search for the divine. When Scripture speaks of "God" it uses some definite names derived from salvation history and some names referring to wisdom that are drawn from the vast literature that treated the world and salvation. The Christian God is revealed both in his relations to human beings and equally in his absolute transcendence. God exists in and for Godself, while at the same time he is the creator of the world and the initiator of a covenant. Christian mysticism distances itself from an impersonal god who is totally above every name and who can be known only paradoxically by means of the soul's returning to its center or source, a return that means the loss of self in the Absolute.

Faith also implies that if God has a name, human beings too are personal beings. That means that faith recognizes the freedom of human beings when they decide to take the path to God, and also to understand divine-human union in such a way that the human partner is not absorbed or annihilated but comes to his or her perfection. As regards the question of evil, it is not the result of a disaster that is divided among gods, demons, and one's ancestors. Instead, in the biblical perspective, evil is to be situated entirely in the secular history of created freedom that operates in the face of the unique God. Salvation takes the form of redemption, that is, God the creator and initiator of the covenant, sends his Son both to make amends for sin,[2] and on behalf of humanity to accept God's proposal of a covenant that means communion with God. By such an act, Christ offers men and women the possibility of receiving the Spirit of God who will give them access at last to true knowledge of the Father.

CHRIST

The theological reflection of the fathers regarding Christ was at the service of the spirituality of union with God and spiritual worship that we have just considered. These theologians are called "fathers of the church" both because they were the first to set forth genuinely Christian reflection and because, in the context of Hellenistic culture, they forged the formulations that in a sense became foundational regarding the reality of God and the truth of Christ. Their theologies are called "mystical," and

---

[2] In terms of the world of cult at the time, to make such an amendment would be thought out in terms of a sacrifice of expiation (see glossary).

this spiritual intention of theirs profoundly influenced the way in which they read the Scriptures and how they interpreted the cultural forms of their times. Their theologies stress the conviction that Christ is the unique mediator of truth and salvation who makes union with God a possibility for humans. There is, of course, a pronounced polemical dimension in their thought: No "extra-terrestrial,"[3] however good (though most were thought to be malevolent), can pretend to bring humanity home to God. Christ can do it—and that constitutes the essence of Christianity. The teaching of the fathers that Christ is truly God and human was the way in which they accounted for how Christ fulfilled his mission as the exclusive mediator and what Christian worship meant.

Today, we are stunned by the claim of Jesus' divinity, but this was not the case at the time of the fathers. Every culture, both pagan and Jewish, turned toward "the beyond," and in circles influenced by Platonism, toward the "One Above." This, too, is how they tried to make sense of Jesus' resurrection. Henceforth, Jesus dwells in the realm of the divine. The words of the Apostles' Creed invoke the powerful image culturally ready at hand: "He ascended into heaven and is seated at the right hand of the Father." Furthermore, they had little difficulty admitting the same of Jesus' human origins: Jesus was divine from the very beginning, as he was at the end, and so, naturally, his conception, too, was exceptional: he was conceived virginally in the womb of the Virgin Mary. But one point especially created a problem. Was it necessary to claim that in order for Christ to be "divine," he had to be "God" in a real and proper sense? But this question gave rise to yet another: If one answered affirmatively, was it then possible to attribute true and full humanity to this divine being? The church's belief answered both questions affirmatively. Jesus is really and properly the Son of God, equal to the Father, and, on the human level, he is "only a man, nothing more."[4]

---

[3] I have chosen this expression, so popular in our current vocabulary, to retrieve something of the thought world of the church fathers who understood themselves to be surrounded by myriads of invisible beings.

[4] This wonderful formula does not come from the fathers but from St. Francis de Sales (1567–1622), who used it in a letter dated November 2, 1607, addressed to Jeanne de Chantal to explain his own humanity on learning of the death of his little sister, Jeanne de Sales. Jeanne died suddenly while entrusted to the care of Jeanne de Chantal. So appropriate is it, that I have applied it to the same humanity possessed and lived out by Christ.

Conversely, to look at these issues negatively, we might say that if Christ is not God, he cannot lead us to *God,* whereas if he is not human, he cannot lead *us* along the path to God. This explains why so many authors between the fourth and twelfth centuries investigated this basic Christian doctrine, and why so many councils[5] fixed formulas that they judged to be as correct as possible to express it. We should also note in passing that it took longer for the church to recognize the full humanity of Jesus, at least in the terms that were available to them (from 451 to 681 C.E.), than to acknowledge his true divinity (from 325 to 431 C.E.). Therein lies a matter to ponder! And finally, Christ the mediator is also the sole priest of the spiritual worship that the true God expects of human beings. At the same time, Christ is the only sacrifice, offered on the cross by the giving of his life. Because the liturgy is exclusively Christian, it is the true path to union with God.

UNDERSTANDING THE SCRIPTURES

The fathers of the church used their interpretation of the Scriptures as the primary way to express the mystery of Christ. They did this by reading them in the light of the primacy of union with God and the purity of spiritual worship. This perspective afforded them the opportunity to impart meaning to the sacred texts, even to those texts of the Old Testament whose literal meaning at first glance seemed foreign to expressing the mystery. Each and every passage was open to an allegorical sense, that is, the reader was able to understand the message of Jesus Christ, the sole way to God, in a variety of meanings. One way was called *tropological* and it sketched out the moral life of the Christian in search of God. Another was the *anagogical* and it encompassed an understanding of the invisible reality of God as one's goal and that words can only suggest. On the other hand, when the focus was on the human being as the one reading Scripture, other activities took precedence. Was *reading* the text or *meditating* on it in order to seize the message what was primary? Or was it *praying* in response to the message? Or again, *contemplating* the text by which the reader almost touched the mystery and took up the anagogical meaning? Theology is first and foremost the reading of Scripture in the light of the Spirit of Christ, in order to gain a "knowledge" beyond what the words themselves can express.

---

[5] The term "council" points to a gathering of bishops at which they exercise their authority to teach and to govern the church.

In the same way, Christian worship is spiritual. First of all, as Jewish worship was, it too is addressed to the One God. Secondly, it does not admit any other mediation beyond Christ's. And finally, Christian worship is spiritual because the only reality that pleases God and can be the object of a symbolic cultic offering is human existence itself, that is, a life of justice and love, a life led in accordance with the gospel and in union with Christ the savior, and a life lived under the influence of the inspiration of the Spirit who comes from the Father. This is the spirit in which the Christian rites must be celebrated, otherwise there is the risk of falling again into idolatry.

THE DIVINE NAMES

With the help of just such precise definitions,[6] the theology of the fathers of the church is essentially a way of contemplation. Their theology is an attempt to delineate the steps by which men and women can hope to be reunited with God. That is why patristic theology pays such close attention to the names for God. The Bible itself names God, and the fathers, who were seeking union with the One who is so named, were led to weigh the signification and the scope of the divine names. Some take a negative formulation—"infinite" (without limits), "immense" (without measure), and "incomprehensible" (beyond the grasp of human reason). Some are often proposed in the Bible and have a metaphorical meaning— "refuge" and "rock." Words like these far exceed what they can suggest to the human imagination and spirit. Others, again, are attributed to God and take on a positive meaning—"good," "true," "Father," and "Son." Still, the precise meaning of such terms must be carefully determined, since they apply to the divine words that first express finite reality. And what has been said as regards the names for God applies equally to the names attributed to Christ. Here, too, we must reflect on the fact that ultimately in God the Spirit is the One without a name.

The steps we take in our search for God are not only intellectual ones, but they demand asceticism also. *Catharsis* or purification was a given in the Hellenistic culture of the time. The task of the fathers was to analyze, discern, and order the practices which men and women used to combat their passions and to transcend their all-too-human ideas in order to be

---

[6] The meaning of such terms and definitions, however, can never be simply taken for granted. They demand constant attention and vigilance.

reunited with God who exceeds both what is experienced through the senses and what can be known by reason. In this case, the fathers by and large turned to the morality found in the Jewish and Christian Scriptures, as well as in the forms of wisdom found in Hellenistic thinkers.

THE CONTRIBUTION OF PHILOSOPHY

With all the required caution when considering the divine names, the fathers felt the need to have recourse to properly philosophical language in addition to the language of Holy Scripture in order to accomplish the task of speaking about Jesus Christ as the sole mediator on the way to mystical union and in celebrating true worship in the Spirit. In the context of the Hellenistic culture of the day, the church had to be able to express and defend the basic faith in One God that it had received from Israel. At the same time, it had to speak of Jesus as the Son of God and the Son of Man, if it was to express his unique mediation on behalf of human beings in search of salvation. In order to face this dilemma, it forged the concept of "consubstantiality," a word that means to say that the Father, Christ, and the Holy Spirit are only one unique and divine "substance." Moreover, in Christ there coexists in a mysterious way this unique divine "substance" and a particular human "substance." With this insight, there developed a whole metaphysical and anthropological quest. On the one hand, this search allowed thinkers to distinguish certain realities without separating them, realities signified by the words "person," "nature," and "essence," while on the other hand, they could refine concepts like "soul," "body," "will," and "action" in order to state the fullness of Jesus' humanity.

Thus, a number of consequences resulted from the need to speak of Christ as Christian revelation dictated. The first pertained to the idea of God, who had to be thought of as one and plural.[7] The second pointed to the understanding of the human, whose structures of being and action had to be finely tuned. The Christianity of the fathers did not shy away from doing for its own culture what it had done with the Jewish Scriptures. It had recourse to ideas borrowed from the philosophy of the day, but it so transformed them in their depths that it enriched the intellectual patrimony of Western culture. In this way, it fostered an original encounter between the inspired texts of the Scriptures and the

---

[7] In recent years, theologians refer to God in the terms of both radical unity and plurality as the "immanent Trinity" (see glossary).

intellectual resources of Greek philosophy. Nevertheless, the synthesis that was formed was not envisioned as definitive or closed. Still, they knew that the Christian mystery could not be announced effectively at this period without both Scripture and philosophy.

The Way to Orthodoxy

Patristic theology, at once mystical and liturgical, gave rise to speculative or doctrinal reflection, as if Christianity was meant to engender the possibility of speaking objectively about God, the human being, and the world, as well as acknowledging each person's place and value in the scheme of things. But this gives rise to a certain number of questions, among which is the issue of the coherence of the two languages used—the language of the culture and that of the Scriptures. For example, how do we reconcile the concrete language of St. John regarding the Word and human flesh with the abstract terms of dogma, such as "person," "essence," and "nature"? It would appear that a certain pluralism of languages must be accepted, with each language shedding its own light on these difficult matters but without exhausting everything that can be said. Moreover, these different languages are shown to be valid and mutually sustainable in terms of the mystery being studied. Each language retains its value in the face of mystery's inexhaustible truth.

The second problem has to do with the choice of cultural expressions for speaking truthfully about the revealed mystery. For instance, in the fourth century, endless discussions were carried on as to whether the Word must be said to be "consubstantial with the Father," or to be "of a similar essence to the Father's," or simply to be "similar" to the Father. Some of the linguistic expressions used by the fathers of the church took on an aspect of excluding other terms, since in their view these words were the exclusive way to truth. A dubious expression can only distort the way to union with God and hence to salvation. The birth of dogmatic vocabulary also led to the emergence of often ferocious controversies regarding the different nuances in a language. It forced choices between the various formulas proposed. The dogmas of antiquity demanded orthodoxy[8] and

[8] "Orthodoxy" literally means a "correct opinion" as opposed to an "erroneous opinion." Here and throughout my treatment, the words "orthodox" and "orthodoxy" are opposed to "heresy" or "heretic." They do not intend any reference to the Orthodox churches of the East.

outlawed heresy[9] because they presupposed an almost direct correspondence between the human word that had been forged with great difficulty and the mystery it tried to elucidate.

Finally, what value did these Christian writers attribute to the culture that was theirs and whose thought forms and linguistic resources they employed to announce the mystery of the faith? On this point, we can say that the fathers drew on the philosophical fund available to them in much the same way as they used the Old Testament: they saw Christianity as their fulfillment. In a sense, then, the writings of philosophers and the books of the Jewish Scriptures were understood to have lost to some extent their independent value. In a manner of speaking, once these "seeds" of the Word have fructified Christian thought, they could no longer lay claim to their former independent status. Both Jewish and Greek thought lost their autonomy and could no longer be considered equal partners in dialogue. The spoils of the Greeks, like those of the Jews, were thought to have assumed new glory in Christianity.

In sum, then, we can say that in the ancient church there is a problem of the coexistence of three points of departure: a spiritual starting point that envisions union with God who transcends everything, and in particular, who cannot be fully grasped by human language; a cultic starting point that insists on the mediation of Jesus Christ in a sacramental act; and an intellectual starting point that strives to express this mediation with the help of certain terms considered indispensable for theology. These issues of coexistence between a spiritual and a liturgical starting point, together with the need for dogmatic reflection, of the importance of doctrinal orthodoxy, and of the value of non-Christian discourse have always been part and parcel of Christian reflection. On this point, patristic theology has always made hard choices, yet without succeeding in imposing them in every context. As a result, Christian history shows that the problem reappears periodically and that it is not possible to find definitive solutions that all parties can accept.

The Question of Evil

At the time of the fathers, the spiritual starting point and the effort at theological explanation were inextricably bound up with the human experience of the tragic pain and impotence felt by sinful human beings

---

[9] "Heresy" literally means "a choice" or "that which separates or divides."

as they stood before the claim of truth on them—the difficulty they experienced at arriving at "knowledge" and their incapacity to live in a just way. Israel, too, though in a somewhat different way, had experienced these painful conflicts. More widely, as did their contemporaries, Christians sensed the tragic element in life and had to do battle with the apparent power of fate. From both of these perspectives, Christ appeared primarily as the one who came to rescue us from human frailty. The truth, which we could otherwise not have attained, is revealed by Christ: *he is the doctor*. With his love he pardons our evil deeds and in the act of pardoning us reveals the true nature of evil—sin is expiated and redemption won for us by his sacrifice: *he is the redeemer*. Our trials draw on the power of his own suffering: *he is the savior*. The means to salvation are the ones we spoke about above. First of all, there is meditation on Holy Scripture, inspired by God and the way to knowledge and truth. Then there is the church's liturgy or Christian worship that imparts redemption from evil to us and that incorporates us into the body of the church by way of a symbolism (see glossary) that draws both on the salvific ways of the Old Testament and the specific events of Jesus' life. The grace of the Holy Spirit constitutes the fruit of these mediations that come to the rescue of a precarious human freedom.

At least in the West, the church had to face apparent setbacks. These included the moral failure of Christianity insofar as the Christian faith, which was considered the only path to salvation, did not elicit the adherence of everyone, and there were countless human beings who remained mired in sin, either because they could not or because they chose not to acknowledge the truth. Next, Christians themselves found it hard to remain morally open to this salvation and avoid falling back into evil. These facts led to a certain historical and eschatological (see glossary) pessimism, of which St. Augustine of Hippo (354–430) was emblematic. Thus, even after Christ had effected our redemption, there were many apparent signs that his saving act continued to fail among men and women. Concretely, at least as regards the number of the saved, many Christians thought that damnation was victorious over salvation. The Latin West seemed to be convinced of the impossibility of eliminating this massive failure, and this led to the emergence of a spirituality based both on the complete gratuity of salvation of those who received it as gift and on the need for constant vigilance as the mark of freedom. The Greeks, along with St. Gregory of Nyssa (330–395), also imagined a parade toward the "full depths of evil," but they expressed a strong hope for the universal restoration of sinners at the end-time. For the East, the path of union with God, which they viewed as seriously as the West, took on more serene contours.

The Church

The questions of heresy and evil also explain how reflection on the church and the concrete forms of ecclesiastical practice developed. By choosing from among his disciples a group of apostles whom he intended to have a special role in the church's mission, and by instituting definite liturgical rites, Christ laid the foundations of a structure for teaching and celebrating worship in the future communities, even though it must be admitted that these acts of Jesus are somewhat unclear. In the final analysis, the forms that emerged were quite diverse, and yet the need that was felt to offer remedies for evil and to forgive sins, as well as the need for an authority to define the statements of belief in the face of heresies, led to the emergence among the people of God of community leaders who were responsible for these activities. Two currents of thought explain the accentuation on church leadership. First, there was the need on the part of the civil leaders of the Empire to identify conversation partners having the same rank or status as themselves. Next, the concept of "hierarchy" emerged as an important way of insisting on the originality of an apostolic function in the community. Especially in the various systems of neo-Platonic thought of the era, hierarchies were constituted by orders of beings that were invisible for the most part. They occupied the entire space between the earth and an Infinite-god-above-Everything, and they played a role as mediators. Here below, too, one encountered visible manifestations of hierarchy—the emperor, princes, and high priests. These cultural preconceptions increasingly characterized the theological interpretation of the functions of governing and priestly activity in the church. Yet, one can detect uncertainty as to the compatibility in all of this with what Christian revelation maintained regarding the sole mediatorship of Christ.

Conclusion

From this first period of our historical journey, we can point to a number of lessons that retain their value for us today and that should be a source for rejuvenating Christian reflection. First of all, theology is primarily a "spiritual exercise." Whatever the language spoken or the methods employed, theology is preoccupied with the human existential anxiety of finding union with God. St. Augustine never tires of insisting that the most pious of pagan philosophers could have claimed as their own verse 28 of Psalm 73, "As for me, to be near God is my good." This anxiety provoked the search for understanding and invested the liturgy with meaning. From it sprang the inseparable unity of the three constant points of departure for the Christian: *lectio divina* of the Scriptures, the celebration of the liturgy, and the intellect's search for meaning. In this context arise the questions of a theology that is mystical, or again, spiritual. What transpires when the mediation of Christ achieves its ultimate goal, union with God in spiritual knowledge? Is God the true object of this knowledge? Does one know God immediately in God's own self or in Christ? Does such knowledge lead to the One-beyond-all-naming, or in other words, does Christian mysticism validate or relativize the divine names? Mystical theology never offers us a univocal answer to this question, but according to the times and the persons involved, the accent will increasingly be on our lack of knowing, or, if you will, on an act of divine illumination. The essence of the mystery escapes the control of our human words.

Secondly, the search for Christ opens up two rich perspectives that the church has never been able to exhaust. At the moment when Christianity, following Judaism and listening to the longings of the most spiritual pagan thinkers, affirmed the oneness of God against all forms of idolatry, it claimed the same fullness of divinity for Christ and the Holy Spirit. It affirmed that the absolute oneness of God did not exclude a true measure of plurality. In other words, Christianity did not put a unique and personal God, a God who was designated by a simple name, in opposition to the impersonal and vague deity of the paganisms of the day. The Christian principle is not pure unity, a unity that rejects out of hand all otherness. The Christian understanding of the Absolute is relational, and the word "God" mysteriously implies the names of "Father," "Son," and "Holy Spirit." Over the centuries, theology has labored to reflect deeply on and to speak about this inexhaustible paradox. More than ever before, today we discern the promise in the effort. The experience of two thousand years has largely shown the perilousness of pure oneness. Each and every time it is invoked, it leads to exclusion and a totalitarian mentality both in the church and in civil society. If one is not careful in understanding the concept of divine unity, it leads to saying that whatever is not "one" does not have the right to exist. Conversely, that which is purely multiplex, that which is "anarchic" or devoid of all organic unity, degenerates into chaos. However wrapped in mystery it is, the Trinitarian confession of Christians permits both solidity of expression to what is affirmed and the truth that is found in dialogue. It should not surprise us that the renewal of Trinitarian thought today goes hand in hand with a new openness to dialogue—and it does so without betraying the confession of God as one. The world of politics would do well to consider applying this universal Christian paradigm in its own sphere.

For its part, the confession of the full humanity of Jesus has not reached its term of mature reflection. In Christian antiquity, centuries were needed to clearly claim that Jesus had a soul, a human will, and genuinely human acts, and that his divinity could not be substituted for these essential human characteristics. Later, we will see that we need to attribute other human dimensions to Christ, if we are to claim unambiguously that "there is nothing human that is alien to him" and if we are to claim that he is truly the Son of God. This amounts to recognizing the full humanity of each person, just as he or she is also adopted by God in Jesus Christ. The paradox of the Christological confession, then, is that it already establishes the nature of any genuine humanism. We shall return to this point shortly.

Chapter Three

THE MIDDLE AGES
The Road to Christian Humanism

In an exposition of theology that is intended to be as short as possible, it is necessary to pass over many theologians and to be content only with the most important figures of Christian thought. The need to be brief explains why we must now move from the period of the fathers of the church to the Latin Middle Ages without too many apologies. This period represents an important stage in the history of theology because theology needed to come to terms with the emergence of a new culture, at least in the West, one that was connected with the discovery of new texts of Greek philosophy. Some thought they were dangerous to the faith, while for others they were an opportunity to offer a new understanding of the faith. To stick to essentials, it is said that these texts transmitted the late form of neo-Platonism, that of the Greek Proclus (ca. 410–485 C.E.) as handed on by an anonymous Christian with the name Denis the Areopagite, and today called Pseudo-Dionysius (fifth century). It was John Scotus Eriugena (810–877) who introduced them to the West in the ninth century. In this way the thread of mysticism in theology and its search for unity again came to bold expression. Furthermore, these texts gave impetus to a broader reading of Aristotle, who up until then was known in the West in translation only for his writings on logic. It was Jewish and Islamic scholars whose work was responsible for promoting Aristotle in the Christian West. These scholars were the first to encounter Aristotle, both in the East and in Spain, and they tried to reconcile his philosophy and monotheistic faith;

his understanding of humanity, which differed in both religions concerning human freedom and knowledge; and finally his understanding of the law and of social institutions. The Latin translations of Aristotle meant that his thought and that of his monotheistic commentators offered new possibilities of interpretation and judgment regarding the Christian faith. The thirteenth century in the West opened up a vast construction site of intellectual vitality—vast but also highly controversial.

To obtain an idea of what was at stake, we need to note that Christ was the sensitive issue. Certain differences of opinion came to light, but differences that were not open contradictions of the faith. For some, the central Christian belief in the mediatorship of Jesus focuses more than before on the human and suffering aspect of the work of salvation. This had consequences both for the understanding of redeemed humanity as well as for the identity of the God who saves. For others, the possibility of a systematic and exacting recourse to Aristotle's thought offered new opportunities for formulating the whole of Christian dogma both as regards the Incarnation and salvation. Here again the choices theologians make concerning Christ will dictate just how they will present God and humanity. Let us now turn to these two options.

THE RENEWAL OF THE OLD PARADIGM

Jesus' Humanity in Its Weakness

The general lines of Christian thought that gradually emerged in the first centuries of the church remained dominant up to the medieval period, even though this synthesis was far more diverse than I was able to indicate in the preceding chapter. We might even say that it formed a "model" that correlated so precisely with both individual human reality as well as with social reality that its disappearance was unimaginable. The primacy of the mystical search for God, a powerful awareness of evil in the world and in history, the need for clear and forceful statements of truth, and the emphasis on the hierarchical in society, all these elements were further strengthened by revelation itself and formed a synthesis that has influenced the history of thought up to our own day. They constitute what is called Tradition, and their influence is found, with greater or lesser emphasis, throughout the whole of Christian thought.

It would not be too difficult to write a history of this "model" in the medieval period, and primarily in the Byzantine world. This world is both a geographical designation and a cultural sphere. It is characterized by a sense of mysticism and law, and it is found in that part of the world where the great dogmatic Councils of the first centuries were held. This "type" of thought developed there most naturally. But the claim could also be made that in the early years of the Middle Ages in the Latin West the monasteries were open to this theology and became its intellectual home.

But in the period and the locale we are now investigating, the classical spiritual theology from the era of the fathers took a turn in a new direction by concentrating on the human element in Jesus, especially his Passion. The Crusades were a powerful impetus to visit the actual places where Jesus had lived, but especially where he had suffered and where his tomb could be found. These were now considered to have a special value. This way of viewing Christ, and especially of understanding the relation in him of the Word and his humanity, was now laden with affectivity in a way that had scarcely been imagined until that moment. The prayers of St. Anselm of Canterbury (1033–1109) breathe a spirit of compassion and repentance before the Crucified One, while his theological writings develop a more systematic reflection on why and how our redemption came about. St. Bernard of Clairvaux (1090–1153), too, proved a decisive figure in this newly created space of spiritual tenderness. Somewhat later, with St. Gertrude of Helfta (1256–1302), the heartfelt devotion for the Passion of Christ would adopt expressions of loving attention to the heart of Christ.

Perhaps more than in the past, sinners lived in a world where the unique suffering of Christ was understood to be what saved them from damnation. Sinners lost themselves in the contemplation of Christ's wounds. There was a new emphasis on the love of God and on compassion in a twofold sense: God's compassion for us and our compassion for the crucified Jesus. Saint Francis of Assisi (1182–1226) is almost a living icon of this orientation whose expansion stretched over centuries and that invested material poverty with spiritual value. This can be seen in two important events in Francis' life, when he creates the crib scene of the infant Jesus at Greccio and when he receives the marks of the Passion on Mount Alvernia. There is a world of spirituality and reflection here that will be developed and will change throughout the coming centuries. Although the goal of the Christian life always remains mystical union with God, and with Christ as its constant mediator, the new insistence on the Passion will lead men and women inevitably to a new theological appreciation of the paschal mystery and of its significance for their knowledge of God and their fellow humans. Jesus' wounded humanity reveals, even beyond the fact of sin, something essential about what it is to be human and about who God is.

The Movement of the "Spiritual Franciscans"

The evangelical spirit that so strongly characterized this current of medieval theology was also familiar with certain excesses that marked the history of the period. When the humility and poverty of Christ were so exalted, it had the effect of leading some to deny even the minimal needs of the human condition. Moreover, it also opposed speculation of a humanist tendency that arose in certain medieval circles and that was interested in new cultural values. Thus, under the patronage of St. Francis of Assisi, some Christians refused to adopt the new spirit of the times. They were opposed to the emerging civilization, not only in their concrete practice, but also by their reflection on the intrinsic value of poverty as a fundamental gospel value. There can be no doubt that their reference to the Poverello, the Poor Man of Assisi, in this regard was exaggerated. Francis had died too early to have taken part in the ensemble of cultural values that were still in an embryonic state at the opening of the thirteenth century. Furthermore, Francis exemplified a breadth of evangelical spirit and a human magnanimity that placed him beyond such partisanship. Later, though, when controversies were fomented, Francis' *Testament* and the primitive *Rule* provided support for his most radical disciples, the "Spiritual Franciscans." These rejected the new understanding of the world and predicted its disappearance. They opposed "the gospel without gloss," that is, the text of the gospel in its literalist meaning, to every human expression of wisdom. They became the apostles and the devotees of a poverty pushed to the extreme of almost denying the human condition. They did so out of the conviction that they awaited a transformation that had nothing to do with the corrupt world that was being advocated in the new thinking or the new order. Instead, they waited for the imminent coming of the end-time. Such an attitude led to acute criticism both of the pagan thought of Aristotle and of the ecclesiastical institution. The latter was accused of being in league with evil from the moment that it accepted the new ideology or depended on the world's goods. Paradoxically, such complete refusal of the world led to an alliance of the "Spiritual Franciscans" with both the enemies of the papacy and with rationalist tendencies at the end of the thirteenth century. Here we see an example of how extremes are often attracted to each other.

Saint Bonaventure (1221–1274)

The Franciscan Bonaventure, as a disciple of St. Francis, espoused the ideal and the spirituality of absolute poverty. He cast his gaze lovingly on the figure of the poor Christ, and Jesus' Passion occupied a preponderant position at the heart of Bonaventure's thought. But he was also cognizant of the excesses of those in the Franciscan family who advocated literal fidelity to the first *Rule* and the *Testament* of St. Francis, a project Bonaventure knew to be impossible to live. When he became Minister General, he consciously fought the "Spirituals" within the order. He imprisoned his predecessor John of Parma (d. 1289), who was suspected of sympathizing with the "Spirituals." He saw to the destruction of the earlier writings on the life of Francis, wrote the official biography that was intended to replace all others, and provided the correct interpretation of the Franciscan vocation. His severity in the face of a certain form of extremism, however, never compromised his conviction in the excellence of poverty, which he defended at the levels of both the university and the broader society of his day.

But Bonaventure also shared the conviction of his "Spiritual" brothers regarding the frailty of the world, and he waited eagerly with them for its imminent end. For him, Francis is a kind of precursor sent by God to announce the end-time. It is essential to remain vigilant and in particular to do battle for an interpretation of the environing culture that insured the fact that Christianity would keep its eyes fixed on the cross of Jesus and resolutely guard the pure obedience of the faith.

Theologically, politically, and ecclesiastically Bonaventure held resolutely to the tradition he had received, that of St. Augustine (354–430), who remained the primary referent for the theology of the high Middle Ages, and that of Pseudo-Dionysius, who was known and appreciated in the West since the Carolingian period. However, Bonaventure read these giants of theology in the recent light of the most spiritualist of Islamic thinkers, for instance Ibn-Sina (980–1037) or Avicenna as he was called in the West. The Seraphic Doctor still resolutely refused the more radical changes that were emerging in the world of the European university and he waged battle with every form of Aristotelian rationalism. In his eyes, humans cannot cease to be what they are: creatures that are essentially promised the vision of God, drawn here below to the excess of love, but always tempted by the evil that has taken root in them by Original Sin (see glossary). Perhaps in an even more radical sense, human nature is marked by a certain hybrid quality. In Bonaventure's mind, the human being has two souls, one animal, the other spiritual. In reality, humans are barely capable of existing, let alone of living in consonance with the high status of their calling. Even at the level of the natural process of knowing reality, the human being is in need of illumination by God to know anything properly. Human reason must constantly remain open to this illumination. The human ability to will is so wounded that it, too, needs the powerful grace of the Crucified One. Moreover, collectively Christians need the support of being inserted into a self-assured Christendom and put under the authority of the pope, the one who has received all authority in "spring-like fullness" (*plenitudo fontalis*).

Under these conditions, to restore human autonomy would be dangerous for humans, for the church, and for Christianity. Any ideology favoring this autonomy must be vigorously opposed. Essentially, that meant the thought of Aristotle. In summary, then, for Bonaventure theology is always an itinerary, a spiritual exercise ultimately, just as he said in the title he gave to his short treatise, the *Itinerarium mentis in Deum*. The cross of Jesus remains the lighthouse we need to guide us on our human journey.

ACCLIMATION TO THE NEW THINKING

Human Autonomy

Things were different in other theological circles. To see this, we first need to expand our horizon and examine another aspect of the situation. If St. Bernard, a monk, can be considered the one who initiated the renaissance of the classical view that Bonaventure espoused and brought to such remarkable expression, Peter Abelard (1079–1142), a diocesan priest, was the one who accounted for the advancement of the emerging spirit of modernity. This current of thought delighted in logic and advocated coherence of thought and even a critical way of understanding the world, the human, and faith. Much later, more attention would be given to the human, and there would be the beginnings of a different division of human activities and a different appreciation of socio-religious groups. After the arrival of Greek and Arabic philosophers at the European universities, the signs of such diversification could be seen regarding the nature of thought itself; or in politics, with the emergence of communes and municipalities, or even with the birth of nations; or as regards economics with the development of banking and a system of taxation. From this point of view, men and women were no longer regarded simply as sinners, who have been promised salvation through faith in Christ, and who have been generously invited to pursue the way of contemplation, at least for certain elites among them. Real personal autonomy was now available to them, an autonomy that over time could lead to a new and deeper understanding of the faith, as well as a different distribution of political and ecclesiastical responsibilities. Wisdom took on a more humanistic cast as men and women began to claim it and to contribute to its flowering, a wisdom that determined criteria of rationality in politics, in the area of sexuality, in the use of money, and in the pursuit of war or peace, but also a wisdom that would try to understand humans as belonging to the cosmos and the earth—all of this without neglecting their spiritual destiny.

The Scope of Language

One of the areas of human activity where this new culture began to emerge was what has been called the "dispute regarding universals." The phrase refers to the discussion of the nature and scope of language. What are we referring to when we speak? What relationship exists between the reality itself—something determinate, palpable, and complex—and the words we use to speak about it—words that are in large part general, universal, interchangeable? If the words we use are almost always general, do they have a real referent in determinate things, and if so, how can we express the universal and the determinate in that which is real and in our knowledge of the real? Conversely, if determinate realities impose themselves on our minds, even before we have the words we need to talk about them, what value and what utility do the words that we employ possess?

The numerous and highly nuanced attempts at answering such questions that Plato (ca. 427–347 B.C.E.) and Aristotle (384–322 B.C.E.) had already formulated hundreds of years before, were later transmitted to the Middle Ages by Boethius (ca. 480–524 C.E.). But it soon became clear that those thinkers, who answered these questions by stressing a certain objectivity of the universal (let us refer to them as representing a "realist" tendency), were really preoccupied with the question of the nature of our knowledge of God, of the world, and of law. To a realist, when all is said and done, and under certain conditions, language leads to a knowledge of reality. Other thinkers (let us refer to them as representing a "nominalist" tendency) struggled with rethinking the supposed objectivity of the universal and opted for an explanation that preferred utility over objectivity. Language helps us classify the world. It furnishes us with points of reference by which each of us in our singularity and uniqueness can occupy the world and be active in it, even though it too is determinate and not general. Words, then, are indications of actions rather than signs of knowledge, without totally excluding the latter. During this period, theologians preferred a *modified realism*, which was thought to be necessary for speaking about matters of faith. They preferred that our words truly connect us with the referents of speech, however imperfect these words might be. What we say has real pertinence with respect to the Trinitarian God and the Word Incarnate. Such language can always be further refined, but in the sense that it in fact expresses truth.

Aristotle

The arrival on the scene of Aristotle explains the emergence of this humanism. Aristotle, also called the "Stagirite," was a scientist who was dedicated to observing nature, and it is from this perspective that he can be seen to have broken new ground of thought. He was concretely interested in the world and in the heavens, in how living things were generated and how they succumbed to corruption, in the anatomy of various animals, in the movements of the stars and planets in the vaults of the sky, and in cataloging the earth's elements. He always sought the principles that explained life and movement in these various realms of observation. Step by step, he arrived at an Immobile Mover, that is, at the idea of "thought-that-explains-all-thought," and the goal of all the movements that are more or less harmonious one with the other and that make life possible, in the heavens and on earth. His vision of the world was that it had neither a beginning nor an end. In this ensemble of reality, the human is a living creature that is particularly mysterious. Humans are subject to birth and decline, to life and death, but they also possess language, imagination, and reason. Among all living things, the human knows the complex reality of the world, is capable of developing relations of justice and friendship with his or her peers, can establish a political life for the city, and can dedicate time and energy to the contemplation of the First Principle, that is, the Immobile Mover. In all of this, however, men and women remain tightly bound to the earth, and it is to be doubted, improbable even, that their human activities, however noble they might be, extend beyond death. In Aristotle's judgment, the human remains rooted in matter, and the soul is nothing more than the form of the body. The soul does not survive when the body disappears. That is the measure of human beings; they are noble and ephemeral at once.

Wherever Aristotle's thought took root, whether in the Islamic world or among Jews or Christians, it provoked both admiration and revulsion. Admiration because of its broad scope, the realism of its quest for knowledge of the world, and the correctness of its observations and claims. Revulsion because of its resignation to the fact of the disappearance of the soul in the face of human death. No Muslim, no Jew, no Christian could accept such a claim. But Aristotle was also rejected because of his way of viewing the world as something eternal and because he accepted a view of the divine as totally self-contained, without any relationship to the world outside the Immobile Mover.

It is easy to understand, therefore, that in the Christian world of the Middle Ages, the controversies regarding the acceptance and application of Aristotle's thought were so ferocious. The adherents of the classical spiritual theology, a theology that had been reinvigorated by its devotion to Christ and his Passion, had little taste for this new philosophy and took it upon themselves to emphasize its dangers and combat them. Other thinkers, though, sensed the necessity of squarely facing the question of the relationship of faith to reason and strained to achieve as harmonious an encounter as possible between these two ways of access to knowledge.

Averroist Thought in the Universities

Just as a certain new awareness of Christ's humility and poverty had evoked the excesses of the "Spiritualist Franciscans," so, too, the increased interest in the whole system of Aristotelian thought led certain masters at the University of Paris to recognize in Aristotle the most accurate way of stating philosophical truth and to privilege the interpretations of his Arabic commentators, even the most literalist of them, and in particular of the Spanish philosopher Ibn-Rushd, also called Averroes (1126–1198). The followers of Ibn-Rushd were known as the "Averroists," and they included the likes of Boethius of Dacia (1230–1285) and Siger of Brabant (ca. 1240–1284), who were skeptics regarding the immortality of the soul and the autonomy of human freedom. It was not their intent in arguing for the ephemeral character of human beings to totally reject humanism. Instead, they were dedicated to the disciplines Aristotle had treated and they observed a style of life that was austere and relied on the minimum of things material. For them, happiness was to be found in intellectual contemplation, albeit fleeting, of what can be grasped of the Divine Intellect, infinite and inaccessible. The Averroists were persecuted, of course, but the highly intellectual movement they started was fairly restricted to a few forceful personalities. In the next chapter, I intend to speak in more detail about an alternative to the extremism of the "Spiritual Franciscans," namely, the nominalism of William of Ockham (1280–1349), a decisive thinker in the Western world of thought.

St. Thomas Aquinas (1225–1274)

Two theologians who represented a middle position on issues, and who were contemporaries, were Ss. Thomas Aquinas and Bonaventure.

Thomas welcomed the thought of Aristotle, while Bonaventure opposed it. Thomas was a Dominican friar, a mendicant and a defender of poverty, oriented toward preaching the gospel, teaching, and theological controversies. He was well-versed in the Scriptures and he wrote numerous scriptural commentaries that are valuable to this day. Very early in his scholarly career, Aquinas became convinced of the possibilities of Aristotle's thought in defense of essential points of revelation, and the same applied to Aristotle's most literal commentators.[1] The points of revelation that were uppermost in Aquinas' mind included matters that pertained to the value of God's creation and the autonomy of human freedom. To Aquinas, Aristotle was simply "the Philosopher," and his Islamic expositor, Ibn-Rushd, simply "the Commentator." Thomas was able to intellectually adapt the secular humanism of the Greek philosopher to the very heart of the Christian faith, e.g., as regards the immortality of the soul and eternal life—both ideas that Aristotle himself had rejected. To Thomas, however, the human was a creature of flesh and blood, but also of personal knowledge and autonomous love. The challenge was in finding how all these elements coming from God's creation constituted a unity of being.

To Thomas, human autonomy was the image of God, and the doctrines of grace (see glossary), the law, and Original Sin needed to be rethought in the light of this autonomy. Aristotle's understanding of human virtue was another area that Thomas would draw on to express the idea that human beings were personally endowed with what is necessary for finding their way to happiness, while always remaining open to a transcendent gift that helps realize human freedom and humanity, without destroying them. Aquinas spoke about God with both moderation and wealth of expression, two qualities that corresponded to his understanding of the human as an intelligent and free creature. His discourse on God and his teaching regarding the human made it possible for Thomas to understand Christ with a depth that was uncommon until then. He analyzed the philosophical principles of union of God and humanity in Christ. With this starting point, Thomas was able to offer an extensive analysis of the humanity of Christ, of the theological language that per-

---

[1] Among Thomas' favorite commentators was Ibh-Rushd, or Averroes, whose interpretations were considered to be among the most rationalist of Aristotle's Islamic commentators.

mits us to speak about Christ with clarity and correctness of expression, and of the actions of Christ for our salvation.

We can summarize the effort of St. Thomas Aquinas by saying that creation as a theme of revelation, creation as an act of God but also as an autonomous reality, allowed Thomas to be open to the new culture that was emerging in Europe and to make room for an "integral humanism"—to employ a phrase dear to Jacques Maritain (1882–1973)—one that was open to a rethinking of Christology. At the level of the intersection of secular and ecclesiastical cultures, however, this gain was at the expense of lesser attention being given to the temporal dimension of salvation. True, Christ was studied with an intellectual precision heretofore absent in Christianity, but for Thomas the coming of Christ to the world remained limited to the horizon of sin and the need of human beings for redemption. The Incarnation was not central to the divine plan, or at the very least it was conditioned by the fact that men and women would sin. Consequently, it was possible to understand creation, humanity, and God outside of Christ—in themselves, as it were—and that these realities could also supply resources for understanding the mystery of Christ. This is a perhaps inescapable shortcoming. As we will have occasion to remark later, an understanding of creation cannot converge with an understanding of history, up to the point of forming a single all-embracing synthesis to be grasped by the human spirit.

Thomas' career as a university professor did not include any responsibility for governance in his Order or in the church. He does not seem to have worked out in detail what the concrete consequences of his humanist positions would be for the life of society and the church. Instead, Thomas laid the foundations for a possible reformulation of ecclesial life and of social and political life. In summary, we can say that Thomas' theology sought to constitute an *event of knowing*, that is, to coherently embrace the elements of both revelation and reason, and to sketch a human view of the knowledge that God has of Godself and of creation.

The Question of Evil

In the preceding chapter, we saw that the question of evil is a touchstone for assessing a theology. In the classical Augustinian theology, one finds a paradoxical marriage of such elements as the intensity of the mystical search for God and a certain pessimism about the extent of the effect of salvation. It is not at all clear that the new perspective of Jesus' weak humanity in the Middle Ages changed this perspective very much. As witness to this claim, some point to the renewed vigor of purgatory in the minds of Christians (some would say that purgatory was invented in the Middle Ages), or to the newly placed emphasis on the sacrament of Penance. For all that, the average Christian remained acutely conscious of the law and lived in fear. In the new theology we have described, matters were different. Sin, both Original and personal sins, was seen less in the perspective of its history,[2] and much more as something structural. The fundamental insight was something entirely positive and expressed a desire for human happiness that was ultimately directed to God and included being equipped with virtues that converge on nature and grace. Law, too, was considered less in terms of exercising constraint on men and women than on acting as an aid for their understanding moral truth better. Sin is something that holds human beings back from happiness, maybe even powerfully so. Still, from a structural perspective, sin appears to be a defect in being fully human, since men and women are created good and possess freedom and desire. The subsequent theological tradition simply could not properly accentuate this fundamental goodness, especially when closer attention was paid to the legacy of evil. In fact, up to our own times this inability to work out the relationship would impose a heavy burden on the understanding of the faith.

CONCLUSIONS

Confrontation

On the whole, Bonaventure remained opposed to the popular Aristotelian humanism in the air. He chose not to accept this new spirit in favor of one that was immediately supernatural and mystical, that is, a spirit that was classical at his time. Bonaventure's approach had the benefit of an extremely focused understanding of the centrality of Jesus Christ and his Passion, which was a revelation of the love of God. By contrast, Thomas Aquinas' thought implied both reception and criticism, adoption and transformation of the new culture. The Thomistic understanding of humanity is ultimately far from Aristotle's, because Thomas accepts revelation, but it did respond to an inescapable demand that Bonaventure either did not want to or could not admit. Thomas offered

---

[2] In an historical perspective, one would consider the following sequence: first there was creation, then the appearance of an Original Sin, then personal sins committed, and finally redemption from sins.

posterity a perspective, influenced of course by his times, that it is possible to be fully human, thanks to a freedom created in the divine image and dependent on God. For all that, what Thomas says about Christ, however profound and extensive it might be, remains less central than in Bonaventure's theological system.

Evaluation by the Church

Bonaventure's options regarding the church, too, were more classical and clearly connected with contemporary forms of society and church, and so can be said to have enjoyed the favor of the hierarchy more than the more innovative proposals of Thomas Aquinas. Already while he was Minister General of his Order, Bonaventure was made a bishop and a cardinal, and he was the dominant figure at the Second Council of Lyons in 1274, while towards the end of his life, Thomas seems to have been an object of suspicion, in so far as he was seen to be associated with the somewhat agnostic Averroist thinkers on the margins of the University of Paris. Thomas left Paris in 1272, and some offer the possible explanation of his premature departure that he increasingly fell into disfavor. Only his evident holiness could explain why he was not personally condemned before or after his death. Several of his positions, however, were included in the celebrated condemnation in 1277 brought by Stephen Tempier, who was the bishop of Paris. Whatever may have been the case, unlike St. Bonaventure, St. Thomas never was made a cardinal and he died in Italy en route to the Council of Lyons in 1274. He was never invited to the Council by the pope, but instead was called in the capacity of a theological advisor by the Master General of the Dominicans, Humbert of Romans (d. 1277).

We see in these actions something emblematic. In the church then, and undoubtedly always, there are men and women of action and thinkers who are anxious about restricting the encounter of the traditional formulations of the faith and theology with the novelties of the current culture, which are seen to be dangerous, maybe even erroneous. There are, however, other men and women of action or theologians, who might be called more prophetic and more audacious, who are willing to take risks by rethinking traditional elements in a way that is unheard of. In the church there are members of the hierarchy, especially at the highest levels of authority, who are more aware of the immediate threats to Christians than to the longer-term demands of the needs of the faith and who almost invariably favor more cautious thinkers. This was the case with Bonaventure and Thomas. As things turn out, though, somewhat later the more audacious positions are seen to bear greater fruit than those of the more cautious thinkers. And so it was with Thomas, who was to become the "Common Doctor of the Church"—a title that would surely have stupefied Bonaventure. The church came to rely on Thomas and his interpretation of Aristotle in defending itself against later novelties of thought, not yet evident in the Middle Ages. Ironically, these very positions might still be demanded by a new emerging culture, one perhaps that would also be fruitful for understanding the faith.

Christian Reflection: Setting Off the Human

One final reflection on the Middle Ages. In the first centuries of its existence, when Christianity encountered a culture permeated by a powerful mystical longing, it accepted the elements that were common to its faith and to this human search, while the revelation of Jesus Christ led it to underscore what might be called the "privileging of the human." Christianity made many efforts to do justice to the full reality of Jesus' humanity. However, it accomplished this task without fearing to use human words in fashioning its discourse to express the truth of the divine reality. That was the very point of the Council of Nicaea's coining the term "consubstantial." The language employed by the Councils at this time is surely not beyond criticism, but we may underscore a basic underlying conviction: the ultimate destiny of the human cannot be achieved by forgetting or despising what is human and its means of expression. What is finite and limited is not for that reason bad, and this is true of language also. When it is authentic, Christian reflection is profoundly human. The same can be said of the unity and transcendence of God. They must not be thought of in a way that disguises a mysterious openness by God to the created order.

But that was the case even more in the Scholasticism of the Middle Ages. Talk of the Passion of Christ and the attempts to exalt the blessings of poverty were indications of a new attention to what is human and, in particular, to human suffering, and an indication of the search for meaning at this level, a search that was to be pursued relentlessly throughout the coming centuries. Besides, if the necessary efforts at understanding are made, it is understandable that the emergence of philosophy in an historically different context would lead to an unshakeable emphasis on human autonomy and that it would constitute the necessary foundation of an appeal to a "supernatural" communion of men and women with God, along the day-to-day path of humanity. We have every right to be convinced that human beings are and must be the subject of ever greater responsibility for their lives, and that this conviction consequently makes for a deeper understanding of God and of the person of Christ.

Is it possible to find any points of agreement between our experience of the sadness of our existence and the awesome power of our autonomy? Or again, can we think and live our faith on the level of the constantly changing journey of life and at the same time on the level of decisive knowing and acting? The Middle Ages bequeathed this question to future Christian reflection, and it is a question that we still have not fully come to terms with.

Chapter Four

THE MODERN PERIOD
The Enigma of Motion

A DECISIVE TURNING POINT

Transition from Antiquity to Modernity

The year 1274 can be seen as a pivotal symbolic date in the history of theology. It was the year in which the Second Council of Lyons was celebrated and in which two of the most original thinkers of medieval scholasticism, Bonaventure and Thomas, died. In a sense, the "classical" period of theology offered its best fruits, while at the very same moment the elements of what would later be called modernity emerged, a modernity that in fact still influences us profoundly. Of course, Christian reflection did not pass so abruptly from one world of thought to another, but a cluster of new factors began to appear that invited Christians to a renewal of thought and practices that more or less happened. It is now time to consider this phenomenon.

The Modern Age challenged Christianity in a more formidable way than either the encounter with Hellenistic culture (the challenge of "religion") or the confrontation with Aristotle (the challenge of "wisdom") had ever done. Modernity brought in its train a change in the whole way of looking at the world, at humanity, and at the individual. It forced the rethinking of everything, including even Christ and God (the challenge of "motion"). Earlier controversies had taken place within a homogenous view of the foundations of reality that was common to everyone. According to this way of looking at things, and starting with humans' observations of the sky and their more or less correct ideas regarding the earth, the universe was understood as stable. One could point to the stability of the elements, especially those of the earth, or to the ordered regularity of the movements of heavenly bodies. Such stability seemed to reflect the very eternity of God, which was defined as "the full and simultaneous possession of immutable reality." If the cosmos was understood in terms of location, a symbolism rooted in spatial terms resulted. Thus, the divine was imagined as "up there," and what was earthly (and eventually what was evil) was considered as belonging "here below." In principle, God as creator escaped all change, and on this point both Augustine and Aristotle were in agreement. Augustine never tired of quoting the scriptural verse, "I am the Lord and I do not change," while Aristotle's contemplation of the world culminated in the mysterious source of the world, the Immobile Mover.

In a real sense, time was not a value in their way of looking at the world. In the case of Augustine, time was marked by the primitive sin of our Parents, who introduced disorder and decay into the created order. Our task, then, was to return to our origins, to restore the original condition of humanity that had been lost. Time could not produce anything; at best it could only restore the primitive state of affairs. For Christians, the Incarnation of the Word, his death and resurrection, had accomplished this complete redemption, so that they had only to hope for Christ's glorious return. The gulf separating the events of Easter from the eschatological coming of Christ were mostly an object of wonder: why did Christ delay his second coming? Christians looked for the signs of his imminent return rather than asking the theological reason for the delay. As far as space was concerned, the earth, fixed in its place, was considered the center of the universe and the stars revolved around it with predictable regularity. All of this was seen concretely in terms of the region of the Mediterranean, or at most a bit beyond it, as including certain areas north and east of Europe. The apostolic mission of the church to christianize the known world was considered complete. The ideal was for the church to reach its full geographical extent in the Empire, under the concerted authority of Patriarch and Emperor.

But reality did not conform to this double idea of the meaninglessness of time and Christian unity in space. Even in the time of the fathers of the church there were cracks among Christian populations, so that their history, their culture, and their religious preferences led to divergent interpretations of the Christian mystery. At the time, these differences could only be understood in terms of heresy and schism. Those who were responsible for dividing the unity of the church broke mutual communion and held each other culpable. Eventually, the two great halves of the Christian world, Constantinople in the East and Rome in the West, became estranged from one another. Certain events marked off this gradual estrangement: the consecration of Charlemagne in 800, the so-called schisms of the Patriarch Photius (867), and finally of Michael Caerularius (1054). Each party accused the other of the sinful division, so that each one saw their half of the Empire as constituting the real Christian space, while the other was left to its sinfulness. The storm of Islam, which had its rise in the seventh century with Muhammud (570–632), became the reason for the Crusades. These were military operations with two goals. First, they hoped to reintegrate the places in the Holy Land connected with Jesus' life and the early church into the Christian sphere of influence. Second, they aimed at eradicating Islam, a religion the Crusaders held to be perverse. Soldiers from the Latin West waged brutal military operations without any regard for their fellow Christians from the Greek East, who were considered to have strayed from the way the West thought and believed. Therefore, it is in no way possible to claim that Christians in the first millennium corresponded to an ideal of unity that they had imagined was there as a simple fact.

The change to a modern mentality would take a long time. It began when certain elements of understanding began to appear, elements that would permit men and women to think differently about the same data and to rethink them thanks to a new way of regarding the categories of time and space. Toward the end of the thirteenth century, the notion of unity that governed how men and women lived began to show serious signs of cracking. The Crusades were proving to be a failure, as was already evident with the crusade led by St. Louis IX in 1270. Finally, when Pius II (1458–1464) failed to raise the needed army among the Christian nobility to combat Islam, the permanence of the Muslim world was simply taken for granted—a fact that was evident with the fall of Constantinople to the Muslims in 1459. The eagerly sought after reunion between Greek and Latin Christians, especially in the thirteenth and fourteenth centuries, regularly came to nothing, as the failures of the Councils of Lyons II (1274) and Florence (1445) amply demonstrated.

Finally, Latin Christianity saw its own traditional structures torn apart. The polemical conflict between the emperor and the pope broke the unity of Western Christendom once and for all, despite what seemed to be the victory of the papacy in the thirteenth century. The exile of the popes in Avignon (1304–1378), coupled with the rise of nationalities that fiercely defended their autonomy in France, England, Spain, and elsewhere in Europe, called into question the traditional political shape of Christendom united in faith and structure. The traditional ecclesiastical shape of Christianity would be demolished by the Protestant reform a little bit later. At the end of fifteenth century, the West, as distinct from the Greek world and Islam, closed in on itself in search of criteria it could employ to distinguish itself from the Greek world and Islam, and just at the moment when the Age of Great Discovery would open unheard-of spaces to it. Moreover, the advent of modern science would renew the way of looking at the world and reveal unsuspected powers.

A Hypothesis Regarding Modernity

If by "modernity" we mean this immense shift in viewing things, we can say that we are still children of modernity. But are we coming to the end of modernity or are we entering a decisive stage within it? At the end of classical antiquity and the Middle Ages, men and women aspired to an ensemble that gathered everything into a harmonious whole that was called "Christendom." Today, too, we speak of the world in global terms when we refer to "globalization." This new global world lacks confessional and religious boundaries. It is incumbent on us, then, to trace the changes that, since the end of the thirteenth century, have resulted today in a universal view of things. At the same time, we must try to determine whether there are any possible encounters left between our world and Christian revelation.

My exposition is based on the hypothesis that from its inception modernity has been marked by a contradiction that explains its incredible successes and reveals its growing lack of self-confidence. The positive pole in modernity is the effective and not only theoretical advent of a new way of regarding the world and the human. We might refer to this understanding by the terms "power" and "freedom." The negative pole of these Titanic perspectives and constructions is the inevitability of evil as an idea, as effective oppression, as insurmountable catastrophe, and hence as the interminable struggle with its positive pole. Is there some way of reconciling these contradictions, and can Christianity be of help to modernity?

Stages of Modernity

In the light of my hypothesis, we can distinguish various stages of modernity. The first stage was both *triumphant and wretched*. These two adjectives attempt to express the human being's twofold and contradictory self-understanding under modernity. We discover an autonomy and a power that is always greater than we can realize. This was the result of the scientific revolution initiated by Nicolas Copernicus (1473–1543) and continuing through the political and industrial revolutions in England in the eighteenth century. At the same time, and in the wake of the persistent moral anxiety of the West, modernity experienced the ineradicable roots of a fault: from the confessionalism of the Protestant reform to the pessimism of civil law among English thinkers, the human being's self-understanding, formerly so brilliant and self-confident, now gave way to painful self-doubt. The French Revolution was the occasion of the second stage: *dialectical* modernity. This form of modernity actively attempts to reconcile both opposed extremes, autonomy and evil, by introducing the negative element into the very history of triumphant freedom. The course of events appears as a process of ruptures and healings, in the course of which a perfect form emerges in which the cosmic, the human, and the divine finally form a harmonious whole. Georg W. F. Hegel (1770–1831) envisioned and elaborated such a dialectic at the level of the idea that resulted in Absolute Spirit, whereas Karl Marx (1818–1883), on the level of matter, foresaw a classless society, where all human and material ruptures were reconciled by dialectical development.

These grandiose syntheses, despite their persistent appeal in contemporary thought, showed themselves to be quite impotent at effectively creating in the real world the longed-for equilibrium between freedom and evil. This is the point at which a new stage, *critical* modernity, emerges to distance itself from the first and the second stages by trying to get behind the unbridgeable dichotomy of freedom and evil and recapture the real at its point of emergence before differentiation. According to critical thinkers, the effort must be made to situate reality beyond good and evil, before the emergence of the spoken word, and even before the insights of Plato and Aristotle, who are responsible for leading the West astray philosophically. This modernity, like its predecessors, seeks to express philosophical, political, economic, esthetic, and religious ideas in one all-embracing insight. Friedrich Nietzsche (1844–1900) was the first of a line of such critical thinkers, at once destructive and desperate, and yet filled with the desire to force the emergence of something new. Nietzsche tried to launch off again on a journey founded on more reliable bases, ones that include freedom, time, and being. We are situated, in fact, in this third stage, or critical modernity.

I have laid out the distinctions among these three stages chronologically, but this does not mean that dialectical modernity definitively abolished triumphant and wretched modernity, or that critical modernity has erased dialectical modernity. The dynamism of each stage remains present and plays a role in the others, a factor that makes distinguishing one from the others very difficult. As regards Christianity, it has been shaken to its core by these events. What can one say of the movement today?

TRIUMPHANT AND WRETCHED MODERNITY

Triumphant Modernity

The Nominalist Option

If both historical experience and the movement of thought by the end of the eighteenth century led to insisting on human freedom and its power to determine the meaning of existence (as we saw was also the case for Thomas Aquinas' understanding of freedom), an even deeper rupture occurred with the nominalism of the English Franciscan friar William of Ockham (1285–1349). The English thinker had an acute sense of the uniqueness, or perhaps better, the singularity of each individual human being and his or her unbounded possibilities of action. Ockham expressed his vision of the human with the two words "singular" and "power." These words are so full of meaning that they exclude every element of universality among the realities they designate and that are thought to share similar meanings. Every true word is absolutely proper, and everything that is possible is indeterminate and open. If there are any common nouns and general ways of spelling out actions, they function merely as means for classifying things and of providing points of reference. They do not designate a "nature" in the sense of some objective measure, nor do they point in the direction of predetermined "ends." The term nominalism, then, intends to exclude all sense of objectivity in the use of words, except for the individual real existent. It is the condition, or if you prefer the consequence, of a powerful consciousness of the free singularity of each human being. Every individual is unique and no universal word is capable of grasping him or her. There are no means by which one can define some "essence" that the individual must conform to or that *a priori* orders his or her actions. The field of possibilities is completely open-ended, and humans are free to invest themselves as they choose. Thus, if there is such a thing as theology, that is, a word about God and God's works, and if there is such a thing as morality and politics, that is, words that speak of human conduct, this discourse must be founded on the open-ended singularity of the human and his or her fulfillment. It is easy to sense just how the interest of philosophy and theology will shift little by little from truth to autonomy (or, in the terminology of the period, to "power") and from a stress on the nature of things to the relationships among things.

The New Shape of the World

These are just preliminary observations to a form of modernity that will be founded on the revolution initiated by Copernicus. It is well known that antiquity saw the world as something fixed: on the one hand, the earth is stable, on the other, the sun and the stars revolve around the earth in a circular motion that is regular and uniform. Such stability furnished the cosmic background of theology and anthropology. Still, for centuries the observation that the planets moved in an ellipsis around the sun tormented astronomers. In the fifteenth century, Copernicus discovered that when he changed the geometric calculations, and if he assumed that the earth revolved around the sun and not the inverse, it was possible to resolve the problem of the movement of the planets. For Copernicus the hypothesis was a mathematical one, but for the astronomers who came after him it became a scientific fact that was confirmed ultimately by the experimental observations of Galileo (1564–1642). From that time on, the theme of a world in motion, one more and more deprived of fixed reference points, proved irresistible to thinkers. In effect, if at first thinkers confined themselves to replacing the view of the world with the earth fixed at its center to a world in which the sun occupied the center, with time the universe appeared more and more to be one of unending motion. The title of the famous work by Bernard Le Bovier de Fontenelle (1657–1757), *Essay on the Plurality of Worlds,* suggests an enormous reordering of ideas and images. Today, even if we are not experts in astronomy, we know that the way we imagine the universe is dominated by relativity and quantum theory, or in other words we have a different way of perceiving space and time than our ancestors had.

The Mastery of the Human

These shifts of imaging the world and the effects of new data are the result of calculations men and women themselves have made and reveal to us heretofore unknown capacities of reflection, analysis, and philosophy, as well as technology. The human being of which we speak is not simply a phenomenon of individual self-consciousness who discovers the capacity to say, "I." Already St. Augustine knew this dimension of subjectivity and reflected profoundly on the human experience of being related to God. For his part, too, St. Thomas Aquinas underscored our human self-mastery as moral subjects. No, here we are talking about a collective phenomenon of humanity who is shown to be capable of measuring all things, of being able to step back from the very reality in which it stands, and of profoundly modifying the conditions of life. This new perspective is a far cry from reestablishing the primacy of the real vis-à-vis the human spirit considered simply as one who discovers what is matter-of-factly "out there." Rather, this new way of looking at the human and the world proclaims the power of the human spirit to re-shape the world and transform it. The ancient saying of Protagoras (fifth century B.C.E.), taken up by the Renaissance, that "Man is the measure of all things," is given even newer life in the world view of modernity.

The theoretical expression of this new way of imagining the human being, following René Descartes' (1596–1650) experience of the *Cogito* ("I think") and closely connected to it, is mathematical thinking. Descartes' methodological doubt is certainly open to explanation. The possibility of exact knowledge—in this case of astronomy in place of astrology—calls into question the truth we acquire from sensory perception. Since what appears to our senses (the earth is fixed whereas the stars move) is one thing, while the reality of the matter is quite different (the earth revolves around the sun), truth appears only as the result of an operation of the mind. We have to surrender to a relentless intellectual asceticism of knowing, if we are ever to free ourselves of the illusions of the senses or if we are to become aware of our intractable propensity to error.

The inescapability of Descartes' "I think" (*Cogito*), experienced in the solitary darkness of his room, is what provides this foundation of know-ing. The fruit of this intramental move is without a doubt that it draws attention more than in the past to the significant contribution made by the thinking subject in arriving at truth. This truth can never be a copy, in the mind and in language, of an object that is entirely external. Nevertheless, the price to be paid for such certitude is high indeed. It leads to the discovery of an unbridgeable divide between the human soul, the true subject of thought, and the body, the necessary subject of error. In other words, the "physical," or what is real as known by the activity of the senses, and the "metaphysical," or what is entirely beyond the sensibly real but imparts its ultimate foundations, cease to be directly pertinent. The task of the philosopher is to reconstruct the whole of what is intelligibly real, and to do that beginning with and in service of the knower's claim, "I think." Rationalism of a mathematical form arrives just in time to support this task. It was mathematics that allowed the first astronomers to declare the truth they tried to read in the skies. Mathematics defines the incontestable character of our intellectual operations. Subsequent scientific discoveries have continued to show the pertinence of this level of knowing, detached as it is from the weight of materiality, like the profound truths of metaphysics, but fully in harmony with the capacity of the human mind for logic. Mathematics makes it possible for us to read the world properly and to transform it by technological applications that do not cease to reveal their power and that permit us to progress in knowing and speaking about reality. *Cogito* and *mos mathematicum*[1] are the two arms, the tools, and the foundations of modernity.

After several centuries, we cannot reject the effectiveness of these two foundations, at least at a certain level of human existence, and their powerful elasticity of approach is not about to be surrendered. Today, when we stress the validity of "virtual reality," we are just continuing along the path opened up in the late Middle Ages of the singular and the possible. We construct models and we build scales of things, from which we hope to gain knowledge of the infinitesimally small and the infinitely large. Digital numbers (the manipulation of the binary numbers 0/1) make the production of virtual images possible for us. Instead of attending to sense knowledge, we see an image that originates mathematically and that exists first in our computer before it finds its way into reality. What an enormous journey from Copernicus to Bill Gates (b. 1955), yet within the same world of numbers. Of course, this is a discovery of the mind, but it is also a discovery of our autonomy and our power. Once again the insight of the nominalists about the singular human being face to face with infinite possibilities is confirmed.

The Awareness of Time and History

The evolution of Western culture also demands that we humans come to terms with the issues of time and history. The matter is not altogether new in the world of Judeo-Christian thought. Nonetheless, the early Christian understanding began with the assumption, at first explicit and

---

[1] This Latin phrase, often used by the philosopher Baruch Spinoza, can be translated as "mathematical method." It intends to say that the way we perceive and understand things should try to approximate mathematical reason and its strict logic. Today when we speak of *rationalism*, either to praise or criticize it, what is generally intended is just this "mathematical method" of reasoning (*mos mathematicum*).

eventually implicit, that the interval between Christ's resurrection and return in glory was a time of waiting for Christians. This alone was its value. Some authors attempted to view history in terms of specific periods: St. Augustine in the patristic period, Joachim of Fiore (1132–1202) and St. Bonaventure at the inception and the height of the Scholastic Middle Ages respectively. But these thinkers saw themselves as living in the "era preceding the end-time," and this led them to think not so much in terms of the delay of the end-time as of its imminence. They scoured their own times in search of the signs of those events that would immediately precede the end-time.

Now, however, circumstances are quite different. Even if the essential facts of the Christian faith still constitute the horizon of our knowing, we must also take into account the value of time itself, time as it actually unfolds, since we live in a world where cultural events can change the way we understand the fundamental structures of being and knowing. What is the meaning of these new concepts and this experience of new powers? What are we to make of the criticism that these new discoveries force us to face, criticisms of past categories of thought, of earlier perceptions, and of our former ways of acting? Questions such as these show how modernity far exceeds the limits of science and its possibilities. It opens out onto a new awareness of time and discovers history, but as the history of reason and its accomplishments and the hopes that it nourishes. But there is more. This new experience for humans is not limited to being open to the future but is directed as well to our experience of temporality in the opposite direction. The point is not to turn to the past to live in it today but to rediscover past civilizations, to understand why they came on the world scene, to better grasp their rise and fall and to unravel the meaning of their journey. The answers to these questions can lead us to a better understanding of life in our current world and offer us possible models for living today.

This broader way of looking at times past can also open us up to the better use of space today. The Age of Discovery at the end of the fifteenth century effectively removed countless boundaries to human experience and knowledge. This, too, is an aspect of humanistic reason, bound up with the realization of historical change ever since Jean Bodin (1520–1596) and Giovanni-Battista Vico (1668–1744), to name but two. We detect the emerging contours of what later the nineteenth century will call "evolution." World history can be understood as the harmonious development of time as duration: time as beginning insignificantly but characterized by a relentless dynamism that tends toward a climax—this latter being hard to imagine and define. Such an understanding of duration is first of all characteristic of the universe, but then of the earth and of the various orders of reality: minerals, vegetables, and human beings and the multiplicity of their cultures. Everything has meaning, or as Pierre Teilhard de Chardin, S.J. (1881–1955) has said, everything is governed by the "principle of complexity-consciousness."[2] What is important for surviving is to discern this meaning and operate within it. The past is susceptible of being understood as a slow process of the emergence of rationality, brought about by certain immanent laws that we can try to determine, and which define the notion of progress as promising for the future. What we cannot discern or understand today we will be able to comprehend tomorrow, thanks to our ever-growing competence and our rational abilities.

The Social Contract

These competencies also play an active role in the areas of politics and society. Those who experience themselves in terms of Descartes' "I think" must be equal in principle, in terms of their freedom and the possibilities open to them. The life of a country can no longer depend on hierarchies that are bound to a static conception of reality. According to modernity, a country can only be founded on a social contract as reasoned to by free and equal individuals. The "republic" that results from such an agreement among equal persons should lead to the best government. Even if the experience of a republic is temporarily disappointing, the idea of constitutional government has been assured. Likewise, the best social order will be the most rational. This conviction is the foundation of the birth and the growth of the bourgeoisie, which is not characterized by something sacred or hierarchical but by one's rational capacity, one's technical competence, and a productive economy. In the area of economics, mathematics once again has played a vital role to the extent that it has helped to extend the reach of economics, especially by expanding the system of borrowing and lending money. In this very concrete area of social activity, modernity proves its unassailable prominence, at least in so far as it remains grounded in technical progress and on the banking system.

[2] On this principle, see Teilhard de Chardin, "The God of Evolution," *Christianity and Evolution,* tr. René Hague (New York: Harcourt Brace Jovanovich, 1971), pp. 237–43 [translator].

Theology that is Rational

The picture that emerges from this brief presentation of modern times is one in which the human is preeminent. In such a humanistic perspective, it is difficult to understand the notion of salvation. If "Man is the measure of all things," what does he or she need to be saved from? True, there is still human suffering, the slow pace of progress, and deficiencies that need to be attended to. As for evil, every period has to face it, of course, but it is possibly more of a challenge to humanity just when it becomes aware of its power to decide human affairs. But modernity considers these reservations provisional accidents that will be removed and that we should not dwell on unduly, even if we run the risk of eventual harsh reminders to the contrary. Modern human beings have little idea about how to deal with weakness.

We call "evil" the slowness of our pace along the path to progress and our impatience with it, or the inevitable reverses we encounter and which we admit are necessary if we are going to march forward. Or again, speaking of human beings, "evil" can be found in our more or less corrupt actions, but we can imagine ways to explain them, and in doing so find our way back to the right path by employing procedures that purify us and correct our ways. We find terms like "sin" and "salvation" hard to situate in our view of things. That is why they have survived in areas less affected by the new ideas of modernity and more in areas that are concerned with discovering the deeper sources of spiritual interiority and of evangelical spirituality. We will return to this theme a bit later when we speak about the Protestant reform.

Surprisingly, with very few exceptions, the thinkers of modernity, even though they have not rethought the idea of salvation, have not rejected God. This can be explained to some extent by the fact that they continued to live in a world still permeated by religion and because they felt a deep attraction that united the human with an Absolute, whatever their conception of it.[3] They had to ground their acceptance of God in a context that was defined by the new way of thinking. The solutions varied.

In the late Middle Ages, because of the accent on singularity and what was possible, an ontological approach was out of the question. One thought of God with the help of the category of "might," and so, was forced to

---

[3] I think of Blaise Pascal (1623–1662) in this context: "The God who is known by the heart and not by reason." This is the opposite of Descartes and clearly a rejection of deistic faith. And yet it breathes the same spirit. It seems that there wasn't any possibility of developing a balanced rationality for speaking about God.

understand God in terms of a power play between God and the human. Later, recourse to the idea of mathematical causality played a role. In a series of ordered and rational causes that make phenomena possible and that seek their "sufficient reason," God is the Ultimate Sufficient Reason of every operation. So pregnant is the theme of causality that it also applies to God who must also offer a sufficient reason to exist. Nothing can exist that cannot be explained by a series of convincing causes, and mathematics provides the model of causality. It follows, then, that God must also have a cause. Failing to find a cause greater than the divine itself, thinkers said that God was *causa sui:* God alone causes God. Only *causa sui* can produce God's very existence by God's own powerful might and thereby offer a self-justificatory explanation of God's own existence. The conclusion to be drawn from this idea of God as *causa sui* is that God, too, must have a reason to exist, even though we are not in the position to provide it. Put another way, the idea of cause is greater than the idea of God, and the most embracing category we can think is that which is rational since even God is known by reason. Baruch Spinoza (1632–1677) expressed the same idea in a different, though somewhat pantheistic phrase. He said of God: *Deus sive natura*—"God, or in other words, Nature"—whereby he meant "nature" as the totality of processes that are the logical foundation of the universe.

In summary, we can say that God tended to be understood at the height of rationalism as the ultimate rational referent, "universal sufficient reason." But because God is "the most knowable," there is the risk of losing the sense of divine transcendence and mystery. In order to avoid losing the sense of divine mystery, we would need other currents of thought for understanding God, such as God as "the totally unknowable"—but this option would probably have the same negative effects as the option of God as "the most knowable." Wouldn't the human being be eventually considered as the thinker and actor in a rationalized world, while in the long run wouldn't God escape the threat of being a "useless hypothesis," as later Pierre Simon Laplace (1749–1827) dismissed God?

With such assumptions, were the theme of Christ's mediation to reappear, it would be in a heterodox way, given the earlier treatments in tradition. Christ could not be called God, because that no longer makes any sense. It wasn't purely accidental that a form of Arianism[4] from

---

[4] Arianism was the doctrine that refused to recognize that Jesus Christ was truly divine by reason of his generation by God the Father. That is why the Creed formulated at Nicaea and recited by Christians states that Jesus "was begotten, not made."

the time of the Council of Nicaea (325) made its reappearance in the seventeenth century. It was called "Socinianism," or more commonly "Unitarianism." A thinker of the status of Sir Isaac Newton (1642–1727) thought the Council of Nicaea was a complete perversion of the faith and that its great defender, St. Athanasius of Alexandria (ca. 296–377), was the one principally responsible for so serious a deviation in Christianity. In line with the idea of God as "the most knowable," Christ would be the greatest Philosopher, the prototype of a humanity directed toward universal love of men, the paragon of a moral life, and sometimes the prophet of the end-time without any traumatic apocalyptic trappings. Jesus' self-consciousness before God and the high moral quality of his life made him the culmination of the historical movement of humanity to find itself. If one retained the term "mediation," it would refer to the spirit of élan that his perfection as a human being aroused in the mind of every reader of the gospel. And finally, a doctrine of the role of the church in mediating salvation became simply pointless. In this view of the church, anticlericalism was far more than a disdain of the clergy in the face of their corrupt actions.

Wretched Modernity

I have just described briefly what can be called the victorious or triumphant side of emerging modernity, even though it continues to be active in later forms of modernity too. Beginning in 1517, the Protestant reform represents another decisive stage in this historical process. At first glance, the Reform might appear to be an absolute denial of the exaltation of the human and the attempt to erase the evil I just spoke about. The perspective of the Reform is found in more traditional forms of Christianity in as much as it emphasizes the universality of human faultiness and thus of the primordial need of salvation. In its view, the modern human being, the unique individual who is open to all possibilities, is really totally powerless when it comes to the most important of human actions, doing good. In order to understand this conviction, we need to consider the Christian people during the late Middle Ages and the Renaissance.

During these periods, men and women were still influenced by the Augustinian mentality of grace and sin, passed on together with the sense of culpability inherited from the paganism of their ancestors and the fear of damnation. Men and women of this period thought of themselves as lost. Starting with the late Middle Ages, the church as an institution had lost much of its spiritual influence, undoubtedly because, at least up to the sack of Rome in 1527, it compromised itself by adopting the humanistic project we just examined. Rightly or wrongly, the people had a sense of the absence of the spiritual in the church and were acutely cognizant of its corruption. And yet the church continued to act arrogantly in pretending to be the sole purveyor of the means of salvation. The church created a climate of fear in the way it administered the sacraments and dispensed indulgences, imposed interdictions and excommunicated the faithful. Its actions were hard to reconcile with the fact that what was at stake was the eternal salvation of souls. The sense of disillusionment extended even to theology that seemed to be outmoded and incapable of providing fresh intellectual, spiritual, and moral guidance in new and trying conditions. Both of these factors led to a powerful spiritual reaction. There were serious attempts to reform the religious orders, while in the world of the ordinary life of Christians an evangelical spirit began to appear. This was made possible because of the new knowledge of the Scriptures that was possible because of their appearance in their original languages, and no longer simply in Latin translation. Such knowledge made it possible for ordinary men and women to incorporate the simple forms of gospel life into their Christian lives. But would this be enough?

The Anti-Modern Reform

The fathers of the reform, Martin Luther (1483–1546), Huldrych Zwingli (1484–1531), and John Calvin (1509–1564), carried people's anxiety about being saved to extremes. The evangelical forms of life at the time were not satisfactory in their minds, however attractive they might be. They rightly sensed the inability of Christians "by themselves" to measure up to the demands of the gospel. Instead, they emphasized salvation by faith alone (*sola fide*). They meant by this that each person, when faced with his or her sinfulness, could not obtain pardon of sins apart from Christ, just as the Scripture teaches. At first blush, they seem to be diametrically opposed to the modern view of the human being: singular and free as he or she faces all possibilities.[5] If the reformers insist on the individual, and so in this limited sense conform to modernity, their accent is anything but positive, since the individual is an incurable sinner who can be justified only by faith. It follows that at this moment at least, God is not understood as *causa sui* and the ultimate referent of all that is rational, but still as the savior God of biblical revelation.

The absolutely foundational character of faith led to what we may call a theological desert in two senses. First, the desert of knowledge. To

---

[5] Shortly, we will see that this is not entirely the case.

the reformers, knowledge shares in the corruption of human faultiness and there is no place for any theological edifice constructed by human reason. This would be a deceitful support beam in the otherwise strong edifice of the purity of believing. The Protestant tendency was to refuse to construct a theology of creation or of glory. Only the confession of the saving cross of Christ can save us. The Protestant is obliged in a way to be an agnostic in what concerns speaking about God but also in addressing the nature of the human and the world. The cross does not give rise to speech. Second, the desert of freedom. The Protestants avoided the temptation of exalting human freedom not only because this freedom has been corrupted by sin and so cannot contribute to salvation, but also (at least among the reformers) because it is completely submissive to the mystery of divine predestination. In principle, the acts of human freedom and the ultimate destiny of men and women belong to separate spheres. Faith, not knowledge, is the strong bond between humanity and God. Knowledge of reality and of the world of change does not give the sinner access to knowledge of God's ways with humanity. Similarly, if one considers human institutions, religious, political, or social, modernity's attempt to place them under the aegis of freedom proves deceptive. Instead, more often than not these institutions originate in positive law, that is, they arise out of society's need for such institutions. This positive law only explains the constraints individuals hold to be necessary in order to live in common, inasmuch as the tragic impact of human faultiness makes them incapable of building a just society. The freedom of faith and the influence of law are the two diametrically opposed poles of existence that can at best be brought into a dialectical balance, never into harmony with one another.

The Modernity of the Reform

And still, Protestantism exercised a great influence on the formation of modernity in general and its religious attitude in particular. In one sense, the decision for faith alone (*sola fides*) when faced with guilt, really bears the mark of modernity. This might appear paradoxical, since the point of departure for the fathers of the reform was the keen awareness of the human sinful condition, corrupted to the point of being totally incapable of any good whatsoever. And yet modernity can be found in this claim insofar as the sense of one's subjectivity is so intensely expressed there. Even if it is no longer the case of a subjectivity understood in terms of Descartes' "I think," it is subjectivity in the sense of, "I am lost but I have been saved thanks to faith in justification given to me by God in Christ." The complete gratuity of salvation, just like the immediacy of the believer's rapport to the Bible, paradoxically has a liberating effect. Luther himself wrote a treatise "The Bondage of the Will" (*De Servo Arbitrio*) and another "The Freedom of a Christian" (*Von der Freiheit eines Christenmenschen*)—without any sense of contradiction!

The Christian of the reform was no longer paralyzed by any religious practices whatsoever. They simply were not considered necessary for finding and walking the path of salvation because salvation was pure grace. In a sense, this spiritual attitude of the all-sufficiency of faith contributed to modernity's estrangement from any relationship to the senses and to what is sensual, both being objects of suspicion to the modern mind. The Protestant mentality tended to push to the margins both the sacraments and all forms of popular religion. The acts of the Christian are no longer performed within the horizon of merits that help orient those actions. But neither are those acts performed because of a "natural law," that is, an obligatory law of action intrinsically connected to human knowledge. Christians are "free" in the sense that their actions are expressions of "living" or entering the realm of "possibilities" and so fashioning their "history." The possibilities of life are limited only to the extent that *in the present moment* certain acts are not possible. It is up to men and women to decide the moral maxims that will provide them with an itinerary for life's journey and that will guide their personal moral rectitude. Provided they do not pretend to ascribe any infinite or salvific value to their efforts, there are no limits to what human beings can decide regarding their actions. In this sense, the doctrine of "justification by faith" entailed for rational and technical modernity a kind of religious permission to set forth on new avenues of action that modern human beings were quite free to engage. If God alone saves us, we are freed to live and constitute our lives as we choose.

As far as concrete human existence is concerned, this approach to life opens up a multitude of attitudes. Happiness in life that is based on the certainty of forgiveness frees one to be fully involved in all the areas of human existence, because they are neutral, or as we might say today, "value free," in terms of faith. Conversely, one is free to choose an austere life, one that takes redemption with utter seriousness and that lives a life of dedication to the interior search of men and women who are completely alone vis-à-vis God. Ignorance of God's ways keeps the Christian alert. The quality of his or her moral life, the presence of concord in one's family life, and success in one's professional life are so many indications of one's being justified by God, of one's predestination.

Paradoxically, then, disinterestedness in the face of theological culture, ancient or new, can leave the believer quite free, if he or she cares to, to pursue the philosophy of religion with all the repercussions this will ultimately have with regard to an understanding of the Scriptures. In point of fact, it is Protestantism that has most developed such ideas and systems of theology, from G. W. Leibniz (1646–1716) to G. W. F. Hegel, from J. G. Herder (1744–1803) to J. Wellhausen (1844–1918), and which has opened up the renewal of theological reflection up to our own day.

Conclusion to Triumphant and Wretched Modernity

The stage of modernity I just described, triumphant yet wretched, presents us with a record of contrasts, rich but lacking balance. Its way of understanding time, its mature appreciation of history and of the power of human reason applied to thought and to productive action, is beyond question and should continue to bear fruit that is beneficial to humanity. The same must be said of the subjective and critical character of knowledge, so deeply rooted in modernity. And still, a twofold weakness of modern theology and a real impotence when it comes to determining political structures that correspond to the novelty of these situations, is clearly discernible in its anthropology.

What effect did the relative eclipse of God as *causa sui*, which had for so long been the guarantee for affirming the subject and for insuring the certitude of mathematical knowledge, have on epistemology? And among reformation thinkers, what effect did the claim of the presence of God, but a God who is both immediately accessible to human conscience and at the same time inaccessible to every human perception of reason, have on religious consciousness? Did these two questions so reinforce each other that they led eventually to the eclipse of God and then to God's disappearance? If human beings can act effectively as autonomous agents *and* observe a demanding moral code, why shouldn't one be confined to that, and otherwise remain somewhat agnostic regarding "metaphysical" questions, such as those concerning the origin and the destiny of humanity, or sin and forgiveness? What can be said of such a significant and unavoidable dichotomy between an affirmation of the freedom of the subject when faced by endless possibility and the lively knowledge of his or her own inherent evil? Doesn't this dichotomy make it very difficult to determine norms that, instead of only controlling evil or affirming the creature's real power, are ultimately liberating in order to constitute a society, imperfect for sure, but nonetheless conducive to a certain coherence and cohesiveness?

Modernity challenges theologians to revise their understanding of terms like freedom, law, and grace. It hands on to us the task of reformulating theological understanding, without denying the genuinely new that modernity has uncovered.

DIALECTICAL MODERNITY

The Return of Theology

The questions we have considered concerning law, freedom, and grace made a pronounced reappearance at the beginning of the nineteenth century. Romanticism, but above all German idealism, was preoccupied with these issues. Briefly, instead of opposing freedom and power, as well as the law and evil to each other, these currents of thought preferred to integrate them in a conception of history and reality that saw them in terms of a process of ruptures and the reestablishment of relations, always with a view toward a positive outcome. On the level of political thought, the experience of the French Revolution was of capital importance. Before the establishment of the Empire by Napoleon and its descent into the wars of conquest of the continent, the Revolution marked the crumbling of an enlightened despotic order and the advent of society founded on freedom. Beethoven's Third Symphony ("The Eroica") and Hegel's *The Phenomenology of Spirit* (1807) agree on this point. The Revolution acts as a "model" for understanding history. It teaches us that history progresses not by way of a painless evolution but by advances and setbacks. In parallel fashion, it shows that human consciousness passes through opposed stages in which the contradiction of one means the advance of the other. At every level, it is necessary to count on a *rupture that constitutes* freedom.

Side by side with the rational appreciation of reality, with its scientific determinisms or its view of historical evolution, one also finds a vision that emphasizes what might be called the *tragic* or *calamitous* moment of reality. This moment of history seeks to take seriously the changes or *mutations* that span history in its physical, biological, and cultural dimensions. The earlier optimistic humanism of "Man is the measure of all things" and the humanism of organic, progressive evolution neglect to take into account the role of *negativity* in history. These humanisms envisioned history only under the rubric of "what has not yet come about" and of the inevitability of progress. Conversely, human beings as subject to law, religious or civil, ran the risk of being suffocated by their sense of faultiness, and the same was true of their institutions. It was imperative, then, to bring out the *constructive power of ruptures* or *reversals*.

In addition to the French Revolution, an event that challenged people to rethink matters, we should also mention renewal efforts among Christians. God as *causa sui,* or the idea postulated by practical reason, or Christ as exemplar of humanity, proved too pale for Christians' consciousness. What was needed was to rethink religion anew and return to Luther's theology of the cross—a theology that was too exacting for Enlightenment thinkers. What St. Bernard and St. Bonaventure sensed, and what Luther had forcefully reaffirmed, namely, the humility of Christ, needed to be placed squarely at the center of theology, less perhaps in terms of the remission of sins and more as the foundational tragedy or icon of human freedom and God's revelation. Modernity's idea of God as the Almighty and as Reason Itself needed to pass through the crucible of rupture to free the negative element in Christian revelation—the cross of Christ and the pardon of evil once and for all. If we know God, our knowledge comes to us only by way of the cross. Still, this occurs in a way that the "order or economy of evil" itself has its role to play in revelation and not merely as something to be expiated or as the price of being bought back, but as a necessary moment in the coming of the Spirit. A perspective that restores the sense of mystery of the cross was to profoundly influence the future theologians of the "kenosis or self-emptying" of God. This theology of the cross is still dominant in Christianity. The event in which God is truly revealed is the crucifixion. When God "empties" Godself, there God is truly found. In some sense, suffering and death must find a place in God, since they are intrinsically part of the dialectic of the Spirit.

Ideas such as these are found principally in G. W. F. Hegel, whose philosophical works tried to restore the human being's real freedom, the true importance of the state, and even the authentic divinity of God. Beginning with the two fundamental spheres of political freedom and the Christian's conscience, Hegel was able to show that they open out onto all of reality. We must be alert everywhere to those divisions that are opposed to a too facile understanding of the mastery of rationality by introducing in the process of reason itself the very contradictions that seem to deny it. *Negative dialectics* is where reality ultimately emerges, even if the variations of understanding are not lacking and create controversy about the proper interpretation. Hegel constructed an immense "encyclopedia" of learning and knowledge. This "encyclopedia" was a theology and a Christology, a history of civilizations, an understanding of the physical world, and a logic. It attempted a universal integration of all reality in which the Father, Son, and Spirit were fully involved participants.

Negation, generally speaking, is not pure erasure. What is positively affirmed remains to a certain degree, but at the very moment it is negated as limited, it can reemerge in another way. Rationality is not done away with, rather it is transformed. What is authentically reasonable includes positing and negating. In this sense, Hegel does not cause thought to arise out of modernity. He maintains the primacy of reason, but develops it in a different "economy," within the greater whole of his vision. Thus, he rethinks religion in the context of an all-inclusive dialectical vision that aspires to include in its movement everything that can be reflected on, and that includes the subject, nature, and history. According to Hegel's way of thinking, the rational character of reality is no longer modeled on mathematics, but more closely resembles a revolution. Everything finds its identity through a process of becoming other and so reaching its true self in "transformed identity," even to merging into the ultimate manifestation of Absolute Spirit, or the reintegration of reality beyond all divisions. The attempt to reintroduce Christianity in an encyclopedic ordering of dialectical thought was open to rediscovering and reinterpreting the element of tragedy in the gospel and so, happily, has moved beyond the deistic rationalism of the Enlightenment.

The return of a reinvigorated Christianity to the broader world of thought has perhaps been too successful. It has taken its place, an essential one, in working out a synthesis that is so comprehensive that it runs the risk of offering an explanation of everything. Are we faced with a new rationalism, in the sense that its explanations leave no room any more for new insights? Hegelian theology gives the impression that it has grasped the end of history. Once again theology needs to come to terms with how it understands the dialectical moment of modernity and how it integrates its own incompleteness in time with the fullness-beyond-time of the mystery it treats.

Dialectical Materialism

The Hegelian system deserves admiration, but in terms of its own principles it seems to have arrived just at the moment we otherwise call "the end of the world."[6] According to the latter analysis, we are approaching

[6] The author is referring the various "ends" spoken of in recent modern and postmodern literature, such as, the "end of modernity," the "end of Western civilization," and the "end of Christianity." For a treatment of these "ends," see Ghislain Lafont, *Imagining the Catholic Church: Structured Communion in the Spirit*, trans. John J. Burkhard (Collegeville, MN: The Liturgical Press, 2000), 25–30 ["Declarations of the Approach of the 'End'"] [translator].

the moment of the total reconciliation of ruptures that is identified with the Absolute Spirit. How are we to understand the historical time that remains for our journey? In Christian vocabulary, we would say that we live in the period of "realized eschatology" (see glossary). How should we work out the shape of the "constitutive rupture" (*rupture instauratrice*) in the time remaining to us? This is a critical point demanding consideration, but Marx paid no attention to it. The German philosopher made dialectical thought his own, but in his view not the dialectic of ideas or of knowledge or of religion but of space. To Marx, dialectic develops in the realm of the elementary and decisive need of the human animal, food, and the means of providing it, work. Before we think, we must eat. Dialectic must be material, and in a thoroughgoing way. Marx did not contest that there are many "constitutive ruptures" that make up history, but they are to be found at the level of the means of production, from the harvest to the most technologically advanced factory, as well as at the level of the relations of production generated by these means. These relations of production result in the conflictual division of labor and come to a multiplicity of expressions: in the pairing of the sexes, between men and women; on the farm, between masters and slaves; in the factory, between employers and their employees. There is reciprocity between the means and the relations of production. A specific means of production will elicit a specific division of labor, then its implementation in turn makes a new means of production possible, and so forth until the time when a state of equilibrium between labor and production is reached that will liberate each individual for a truly autonomous life. The superstructures of consciousness and organization make each of these stages possible and are progressively modified, with the result that at the end of the process they will disappear. The state and religion are such superstructures. The more humanity advances, the more conflictual are the relations of production due to the phenomenon of the appropriation of the means of production. An increasingly violent dialectic emerges between those who have only bare physical strength and those who own the instruments of production and the land, the materials of production and the machinery. The opposition is far from static, nor can we speak of a moral dysfunction. Class struggle belongs to the very dynamic of what is real, so that the moment of the greatest oppression will be reversed by the moment of complete liberation. According to Marx, history is now approaching this extreme moment or "end." The final stages will be the appropriation of the means of production by workers (economic reversal), the dictatorship of the proletariat (political reversal), and the disappearance of the state and the arrival of the classless society (the final moment).

The failure of Marxism as it has taken root in a given society, its incapacity to force the advent of those terminal moments of the dialectic—the final revolution that is always in sight but never actually arrives—might lead us to declare its vacuity as a system. This would be to jump the gun. In reality, the notion of a "constitutive rupture" corresponds to the march of history in a way that can be ascertained. Yes, it deals with the realm of ideas, but it also characterizes social and political life, as well as their economic conditioning. The negating of any specific cultural, social, or economic situation means the emergence of a new state of affairs that both addresses and transforms the old state of affairs, while it is freed to address an unforeseen and always possible future. In other words, the reciprocal nature of singularity and possibility, so constitutive of modernity, reveals a dialectical nature with Hegel and Marx that simply cannot be avoided.

So many questions spring up at this point. If we concede the essential truth of the dialectical point of departure and if we understand that it plays a role at every level of human existence—civil, religious, social, economic, and personal—can we find a way to bring these different perspectives into harmony and define a coherent vision of humanity on the march? The great thinkers of the Middle Ages were able to do this for their time, a time when they saw the world as unchanging, but can we do it for our time?

Given the fact that this desire is fairly universal in our days, it is clear that it would be illusory to construct a system that in principle ignored any single dimension of human existence. The political and socio-economic world cannot count on constructing a balanced view if it dismisses the philosophical, and even the religious, dimension of human existence. Conversely, a renewal of religious reflection and practice that ignores civil matters and refuses to submit to the dialectic of all the properly human dimensions of human beings, but especially the political and economic dimensions, would be a fatal abstraction. And yet, what should be our point of departure? Should it be conscience, or material needs, or something else? And from this starting point how can we imagine the dynamic globally in a way that is not deterministic and totalitarian? Or again, how can we prevent the system from suffocating the individual person? In other words, how can we legitimately distinguish in the dialectical process the structure of guilt and the beneficial negation of social perversion?

CATHOLICISM IN DISARRAY

In this new but long-term cultural context, Catholicism gives the impression of a lack of élan needed to develop a creative understanding of the times. Since the beginning of the "dispute regarding universals" in the twelfth century, theology was conscious of the fact that total nominalism was incompatible with the correct expression of the faith. To speak of God or of the human being or of Christ necessarily meant that there was some universal and objectively grounded element of signification in the words we used. Terms like law, grace, freedom, sin, and divinity must contain some objective content, since without some determinate meaning it would be difficult to express the mysteries of the faith in their fullness. But the victory of nominalism meant that the earlier theology no longer had a place. The humanism of a Thomas Aquinas should have provided an alternative as worthy of attention as that of William of Ockham. But when it came to criticizing Ockham, the tendency was to turn to Ockham's extremist confreres, the "Spiritual Franciscans," who showed no interest in the world's possibilities. They were committed instead to an attitude of waiting for the imminent end-time, which they awaited in the spirit of absolute poverty. Curiously though, both extremes—nominalism and spiritualism—entered into a politico-spiritual alliance with each other.

If the humanism of Thomas Aquinas had been allowed to offer an evaluation of singularity, freedom, and action that was not exclusively nominalist, it would still not have been able to respond to the new challenges of science, at least not at the start. On first view, the proposals of the new astronomers from Copernicus to Galileo created problems because they called into question a fixed view of the world[7] and because they were not compatible with the literal interpretation of certain passages of the Scriptures. The question of Scripture would return later in an even more disturbing way, when, with Richard Simon (1638–1712) and Baruch Spinoza, the process of revelation itself would be examined critically. The transmission of the authentic text was problematic in itself, since the texts Christians possessed contained possible corruptions of the originals to

---

[7] This fixed view is usually associated with the astronomical positions of Aristotle (fourth century B.C.E.) and Ptolemy (second century C.E.). However, it was broader than this since it was extended to include the general view of the stability of things or the question of the limits of change.

an extent that they were not aware of. Much needed to be done to assure that the new culture emerging would be a Christian one.

From the late Middle Ages on, what was needed was the progressive implementation of a Catholic modernism, but the times were not ripe. Throughout the period, since Meister Eckhart (ca. 1260–1328) up to François Fénelon (1651–1715), by way of the Spanish mystics and then St. Francis de Sales (1567–1622) and the French School, there was an extraordinary flowering of spirituality, often regarded with suspicion by ecclesiastical authorities. But the period in question would not permit a new and properly theological formulation attuned to the questions of modernity.

In the first years of modernity, Catholicism concentrated on erecting a monument of doctrine instead. The decisions of the Council of Trent (1545–1563) were popularized in all Roman Catholic parishes due to the publication of its famous *Catechism*. In itself the Council has an intensely cultural and theological significance. It reaffirmed a certain objective meaning to the words used in the statements of faith. It proposed to maintain a delicate balance in its statements regarding nature, freedom, and grace. As for the value of history, while admitting the negative side of human origins, it left open the possibility of hope in the struggle between good and evil. It admitted the value of the world by acknowledging our human senses and the place of symbolism by emphasizing the irreplaceable role of the sacraments.

The Council of Trent furnished certain decisive reference points as guides for addressing the new questions of science and history and for formulating new articulations of the faith and culture. Unfortunately, many drew on the Council to argue in a one-sidedly confessional way. This was particularly the case with the use of many elements of the Council's teaching opposed to Protestantism. Two of the most controversial issues between Catholics and Protestants after Trent were the self-sufficiency of the "order of nature" and the church's ecclesiastical institutions. These emphases found their way into the canons of the law of the church and gave to Catholicism a strong self-image, one tinged by the reform of its sacraments and hierarchical structures. This was to the profit of doctrine and the defense of the faith in the church, but in the meaning that these had acquired during years of stability in matters of doctrine and faith. Traces of modernity—and not the best modern ideas—crept into the Catholic system, such as the insistence on God as All Powerful, usually understood in a way that portrayed God as absolute and threatening to men and women, while human beings were seen as weak, thus leading to a marked rigorism in moral matters.

In any case, the climate was one of opposition to modernity both intellectual as well as social and political. In the Catholic church, no one of the talent of Peter Abelard (1079–1142) or Thomas Aquinas had the audacity to reflect deeply on the new modernity and integrate the old with it, except perhaps for Nicholas of Cusa (1401–1464). Moreover, in the modern era, unlike the patristic and the medieval periods, the church did not have theologians of quality even to defend the classical positions in theology. In the seventeenth century, it was Robert Bellarmine (1542–1621) and J.-B. Bossuet (1627–1704) who followed in the footsteps of Bernard and Bonaventure, and they were far from equaling the caliber of their worthy predecessors.

Conclusion: Critical Modernity

Now is the time to spell out the final phase of modernity or what I have called *critical modernity*. This form of thought is conscious of the inadequacies and the failures of the earlier stages of modernity, the *triumphant and wretched* and the *dialectical*. It tries to open up different avenues of thought. Nonetheless, it hardly seems possible to draw up its record, even a provisional one, because we ourselves belong to this critical modernity, both hesitant and boldly assertive, and it is difficult to synthesize the different paths thinkers who represent this stage have trod. If one takes Friedrich Nietzsche as the point of departure for this critical modernity and as one of its most forceful spokespersons, we must not forget that the renewal of Christian reflection began during the same generation. If its two precursors were John Henry Newman (1801–1890) and Soren Kierkegaard (1813–1855), the first decisive theologians of the new Christian thinking were Nietzsche's contemporaries. The names of these creative thinkers include Maurice Blondel (1861–1949), Adolf von Harnack (1851–1930), M.-J. Lagrange (1855–1938), Alfred Loisy (1857–1940), Vladimir S. Soloviev (1853–1900), Friedrich von Hügel (1852–1925), and Julius Wellhausen (1844–1918)—the pioneers of a lineage that is extremely rich and that continues to our own day in all the Christian confessions. Ideally, I should show how their development is inter-related: from Nietzsche to Paul Ricoeur (1913–2005) and Jürgen Habermas (b. 1929), and from Blondel to Karl Rahner (1904–1984) and Jürgen Moltmann (b. 1926)—how they have come to represent the human intelligentsia in the past hundred and fifty years.

To be faithful to my chosen method of comprehensiveness, I would have to situate this intellectual development in the context of what was happening in the contemporary civilizations. I would have to describe the background of world history, marked by unprecedented technological progress and a succession of more extensive wars, longer wars and wars involving larger and larger populations and greater and greater land masses. These factors have engendered a desire for peace that itself has grown to meet the new technical capacities and the depths of the human disasters suffered. Finally, in terms of the renewal of the churches, I would have to point to the new importance of ecumenism and to the difficult but steady path of the Catholic church toward modernity since Pope Leo XIII (1878–1903) and up to the Second Vatican Council (1962–1965), not to forget the commitment to inter-religious dialogue.

Only one indication will have to suffice for our proposal. Among its secular representatives, critical modernity manifests an undeviating tendency to reject a rationality that is seen to be death-dealing, every bit as much as it rejects the smooth-talking rationality of the first period and dialectical rationality, too, that calls for constant revolutions undertaken one after the other in order to realize oneself in terms of "transformed identity." But why propose anything, or what can be achieved? What would be the foundation on which reality could be built, so that intelligence would not lose what it is entitled to and history would remain open to new possibilities?

Is there another possibility? Does it make sense to go back to a point of origin before all historical process and to search for another way of understanding the ensemble of intelligence, esthetics, politics, and religion? One senses that each thinker of critical modernity imagines himself or herself to be the one who has finally discovered truth. Nietzsche emphasized the discovery of the innate will to power that appears somewhat in a new guise of the singularity of the subject and as affirmed at the time nominalism emerged in the Middle Ages. Besides, he underscored the truth in the exaltation of life before any moral constraints, but also as the awakening of the idea of the "eternal return." Sigmund Freud (1856–1939) has found truth in plumbing the depths of consciousness. Martin Heidegger (1889–1976) finds truth in the retrieval of Being, which had lain forgotten since Platonism. Jacques Derrida (1930–2004) points to the need to return to the pre-linguistic origin of truth. And Michel Foucault (1926–1984) calls us to undertake an archaeology of knowledge and of social life. The examples could be multiplied.

All of these studies are the subjects of pertinent criticisms and excellent analyses. In my opinion, the limitation they all have in common, and that explains their failure and the endless retracing of the problem in each generation, comes from their inability to come to grips with the problem of evil, in such a way that evil not be considered as a definitive obstacle to life or history or being, but on the contrary as a somewhat positive step along the unpredictable journey of humanity. I believe that Christian modernity has something positive to contribute to the search, and that is what we must now turn our attention to.

PART TWO

THEOLOGY IN OUTLINE

To facilitate the transition from the journey so far to an outline of theology I aim to propose, I would like to offer a summary of what I have examined to this point in order to highlight the most important stages along our way. Then, I will propose a hypothesis that aims at answering the central question of all theology, but of Christian theology in particular, the question of freedom, grace, good, and evil.

AN OVERVIEW OF THE ROUTE TRAVELED

In the first stage of the encounter between biblical thought and pagan culture, Christians determined which elements were essential to the faith. The name of God, revealed to Israel as unique, personal, and desiring covenant with humanity, was given to the unknown and vague deity of paganism. At the same time, Hellenism's characteristic mystical desire for union with the divine, and that belonged to "Gnostic" circles in the widest sense of the term, contributed greater spiritual depth to historical Judaism. Jesus is the ultimate mediator between God and humans, in the line of the patriarchs, the prophets, and Jewish wisdom figures. Except for sin, Jesus was human like us, but was ultimately acknowledged to be the Son of God, identical to the Father in divinity. The Spirit, too, whose role is to bring us into covenant relationship with God, is also divine. In the final analysis, we find ourselves challenged by a confession of faith that is paradoxical: God's oneness does not exclude a mysterious plurality of Father, Son, and Holy

Spirit, and this paradox illuminates anew the ancient enigma of philosophy, the question of the one and the many. God is deprived of an exalted transcendence that locks him away in a realm of unknowing. Moreover, the paradox draws humans closer to God when "one of the Trinity becomes incarnate." Henceforth, "knowledge of God" is no longer an impossible utopian dream but a future promise and an already present experience.

At the same time, Christians took care to retain the full humanity of Christ, the Son of God. He must be one of us in every way. This second claim supposes a refining of the notion of what it is to be human, just as the first claim refined what God is like. It is not a matter of a soul having fallen into matter or, speaking in more general terms, of a badly laid out structure whose beginnings defy our understanding. With the human, we are dealing with something coherent, whose body, soul, mind, will, and freedom have intrinsic worth. Christ's humanity reveals what it is to be human *tout court*. The efforts of the centuries of the great ecumenical councils laid the foundations for a humanism that will emerge in the Middle Ages. Human beings are the image of God (*imago dei*) in their very autonomy, which can make room for our unlimited knowing and willing. The only condition of this "imaging of God" is that we humans respect our fundamental bond with God, just as Jesus had done.

In this context of salvation, however, sin continues to play an important role. However powerful grace may be, men and women continue to run the risk of definitively refusing God's goodness by opposing our freedom to it. Our human refusal of God continued to occupy an important place in Christian thought.

A new consciousness of human nature, one marked anew by the paradox, emerged in the Middle Ages. Medieval Christians meditated on the humanity of Christ differently from Christians in the patristic period. Medieval Christians were open to Christ's Passion through spiritual experience that developed in human hearts elements of confidence and tenderness for Christ the Lamb of sacrifice. Such meditation accentuated the high price exacted by sin and the need for vigilance. On the other hand, in light of the new philosophical insights, a deeper appropriation of humanity and its freedom before God, other human beings, and the world began to emerge. Such themes of revelation as the law, human failure, and grace began to take on new relationships to each other. They were interiorized so that freedom was thought of more positively, supported rather than threatened on the path to the knowledge of God. This view had consequences for the understanding of the humanity of the incarnate Jesus as well. Unfortunately, the implications of this new view of being human were not fully accepted at the time, so that the understanding of autonomy in the domains of politics and society did not receive the justification it should have been accorded.

Modernity, which appeared at the start of the fourteenth century, at first very slowly but then more quickly, showed signs of a twofold development. First, the view of the cosmos lost its appearance of fixity or stability. Second, the experience of society began to become more secular, with political and financial institutions distancing themselves increasingly from religious institutions. The extent of scientific discoveries and the extension of technical abilities tended to place human beings more and more in the forefront and to perceive time and history as constitutive dimensions of reality and of knowledge. In truth, this perception was in continuity with the historical dimension of Judeo-Christian revelation, and in the long run was to serve better the understanding of Christian faith. The task began to loom large on the horizon that thinking through the coherent message of Christianity, or at the very least the way it accounts for itself, was inescapable. How could Christians reconcile the understanding of the faith that issued from the stable and mystical world of the first millennium, aided by Greek philosophy and the various reinterpretations of Judaism, Christianity, and Islam, with an understanding demanded by the new paradigm centered on the human and history?

In the short term, modernity reacts to the human paradox at every stage of Christian reflection in a way that is almost contradictory. On the one hand, the singularity of the subject that was highly emphasized by nominalism recognizes no limits to the application of human power; while on the other, the urgent experience of evil forces an insurmountable dialectic of ever-present failure and of a pardon that is at the same time complete and incapable of restoring dignity to human beings. Men and women, at once too powerful and too evil, struggle to understand the meaning of God's revelation in Jesus Christ in the new context of their changed civilization. They are also hesitant about implementing the positive and balanced structures appropriate to the state, society, work, and the use of money. What results in the concrete development of humanity is a growing disequilibrium between the triumphs of science and technology and the evil that humanity and the world experience, and that is manifested in the many forms of violence that appear without abating.

Looking at matters from another perspective, one can say that the expansion of humanity's capacity of analysis and the powers that correspond to it, had paradoxically engendered a loss of contact with what is real to our senses—qualities, colors, shapes—to the benefit of an abstraction that continues to grow unchecked. Do the impressive results of this abstractive ability compensate for the always progressive estrangement from our senses? And do we not find a place anymore for the realm of the "metaphysical," or what we might today call the "meta-numerical," for "essences" that at bottom are the reason of the ultimate being of phenomena that are always better produced and controlled at the same time? Deprived of a living articulation of what is *sensed* and of what is *essential,* modern men and women run the risk of abandoning themselves in their leisure time on the one hand to sensuality, while on the other to the esoteric. What is needed to restore a balance of thought and life, in a world of motion and competence, without denying the one or the other but by clearing the proper space for the "thickness," as it were, of the flesh and for the varied levels of transcendence?

Since the Middle Ages the importance of the cross continued to grow in the sensibilities and minds of Christians and provided the key to open the Christian mystery to history during the period I have called dialectical modernity. In the cross, the very contradiction between the power of freedom and the inventiveness of evil is lived and overcome. In effect, this contradiction is not a static opposition between limited values but a process. Freedom itself happens only by agreeing to pass by way of what seems, and to some degree is, its negation by means of which it can grow and confront new space. In this sense, the cross of Christ is the key to interpreting history and the place of the revelation of God's very self. In the more static perspective of the classical period, what were thought to be "subsistent relations" at the very center of oneness, in modernity were thought of in terms of an infinite dialectic. God exists in an intimate history of freedom and gift. This is surely the direction in which we must go, but in such a way that it leaves a large margin for speaking about the Incarnation.

A HYPOTHESIS: DESIRE, TRAGEDY, AND "TRAGIC MISFORTUNE"

In order to move forward on the path I have just summarized and the problems it raises, I propose at this point to make a distinction in the matter of the interplay between freedom and the endless possibilities open to human beings. I propose to distinguish between *"tragedy"* (*la tragédie/tragique*) and *"tragic misfortune"* (*le drame/dramatique*) against the background of *desire.*[1] If thinkers are not in agreement about the nature

---

[1] My remote inspiration for employing this terminology is found in Jean Anouilh's (1910–1987) description of *tragedy* that is "clean and at rest," and *drama*

and the conditions of happiness, nevertheless they do agree that what tends toward happiness (knowledge, love, action, enjoyment) constantly leads human beings toward *desire*. I will call the conflict of desires that is at the root of all human community *tragedy*. The subject's desires are good and, in a sense, unlimited. As modernity so well understands, there is freedom and there are possibilities. But the desires of one subject necessarily collide with the desires of another (or of many others), and reaching agreement among them is not easy. Often, one person will spontaneously be in conflict with another, and the only way to resolve it is by consent. Paradoxically, the way to realize one's true self, apparently the primary object of desire, is by forming a "we." The resolution of such a conflict presupposes a *desire for communion*, or love that is stronger than our personal desires to know, achieve, enjoy, etc. At a first level, "suffering," "renunciation," and "death" would be natural and unavoidable stages that are not characteristic of failure but of the encounter of innocent persons who must renounce themselves in order to be united with each other. They belong to paradise and are not an antechamber of hell. They illustrate the axiom that says that to love is to give one's life for those one loves, and in turn, to receive love from them. To return to the fundamental categories of modernity, instead of speaking about "freedom and the possible," we must speak about "freedom, *the other*, and the possible."

---

that is "soiled and ignoble." [Translator's note: The quote by Anouilh is as follows: "[Chorus] Nice and neat, tragedy. Restful, too. In a drama, with its traitors, its desperate villains, its innocent victims, avengers, devoted followers and glimmers of hope, death becomes something terrible, a kind of accident. You might have arrived in time with the police. But tragedy's so peaceful! For one thing, everybody's on a par. All innocent! It doesn't matter if one person kills and the other is killed—it's just a matter of casting . . . And above all, tragedy's restful, because you know there's no lousy hope left. You know you're caught, caught at last like a rat in a trap, with all heaven against you. And the only thing left to do is shout—not moan, or complain, but yell out at the top of your voice whatever it was you had to say. What you've never said before. What perhaps you didn't even know till now . . . And to no purpose—just so as to tell it to yourself . . . to learn it, yourself. In drama you struggle, because you hope you're going to survive. It's utilitarian—sordid. But tragedy is gratuitous. Pointless, irremediable. Fit for a king!" See *Antigone*, trans. Barbara Bray (New York: Methuen Inc., 1987) 102. In order to bring out the added dimension of misfortune or calamity involved in the French *le drame* (which Anouilh points to and which Lafont builds on), I have preferred the translation "tragic misfortune."]

On the contrary, I call "tragic misfortune" situations that result from the refusal to consent to communion, in other words the refusal of those shifts in conduct that are necessary for building communion, all because I mistakenly imagine that I must always affirm myself (the "One") to the exclusion of the other. What results is a wound, and not only at the level of personal injury but also of damage to one's environment (the body and the world), because it is always out of concrete factors that the conflicts, instead of being resolved, fester. In what I call "tragic misfortune" are found fault, culpability, woundedness, death—partly irreversible. History is made up of the tragedies that have come our way, and which we've accepted or refused to accept, of situations of "tragic misfortune" that have befallen us, and of the hurts that have compounded the situation. In other words, "tragic misfortune" is the refusal of death that is inherent in tragedy and that is creative. Instead, one falls prey to the sacrificial slaughters of "tragic misfortune" and its element of negativity which contributes nothing. In the face of situations in life marked by "tragic misfortune" the only solution is *forgiveness*, which reestablishes communion and opens the way to a difficult and costly restoration of the damaged world.

In my opinion, with the "categories" of desire, tragedy, "tragic misfortune," and forgiveness—all of which are pertinent for speaking of interpersonal exchange, for exchange with God, and possibly for God himself—we have the key for understanding and acting that highlights freedom and the possible, those fundamental values of modernity. At the same time, we are able to escape the suffocating power of evil that leaves us without hope, and that neither Luther nor Hegel were able to exorcise from the world. A door is opened to Trinitarian faith. Because *God is love* he does not jealously claim his infinity but incessantly and in all situations offers himself in exchange. In addition to the light of love, we might also be able to progressively bring out a new understanding of what it is to be human: to be *free*, but not in the sense that modern subjectivism would have it, and *corrupt*, but not as the Protestant reform thought or simply as a pagan pessimism latent in us would have us believe either. And finally, we could regain the "physical" (in the sense of reality open to our senses) and the "metaphysical" that are hidden and so mistakenly rejected. In this way, the classical and the modern way of understanding human being can be rearticulated and a new or well-grounded hope can become a possibility.

Chapter Five

TIME AND DIVINE COVENANT

Having completed our excursion through history, we understand better that the point of departure for all reflection on Christ in the New Testament is the "paschal mystery." We must never stray from this foundation—the death and resurrection of Christ that we "remember" and whose meaning we search for. Christian reflection in all its forms can be characterized as an infinite series of variations on the death and resurrection of Christ. Throughout the centuries, these variations were dominated by the theme of redemption as victory over evil. But today we are conscious of the fact that death and resurrection have a more radical meaning, and that is what we must now try to elucidate.

CHRISTIANITY AND A SPACE FOR MEMORY

Christianity understands itself as a space for remembering. It recalls the death and resurrection of Jesus and waits for his return which will be a blessing for all humanity. Christianity implies an understanding of time that is worth the effort to spell out, however briefly.

First of all, Jesus lived in time as we experience it. He belongs to our history and an unbroken thread ties us to him, as is the case with all other historical personages. This thread also ties him to the multitude of those nameless men and women who have existed since human beings first appeared upon earth. Jesus lived the greater part of his life in the ordinary situations of work, family life, and proximity to others. He also lived against the backdrop of the actual politics of his day, and within the sphere of the religious observances of his people as enunciated by the Scriptures. Jesus, in other words, lived under the covenant of God with Israel. At last, he left his ordinary milieu in order to dedicate himself over the course of two or three years to proclaiming God's kingly rule. This meant that he announced the end of time as we humans know it and its transformation. He prepared his contemporaries for this end by revealing God's ultimate plan for time. His message was refused and he died as a consequence of the rejection. Jesus' death, then, has a double aspect. It is the rupture with time, which is the fate of every human being, and it was a tragic event bound up with a religious conflict in which God had a role to play. In this respect, the death of Jesus has a quality of surprise. Though he was God's messiah, God who sent him did not stand by him at the end, as he was dying. Was he indeed who he pretended to be? If he was an impostor, his message and his life's work were really unimportant. If he was who he claimed to be, what possible understanding of this God can we form, a God who sent him on a mission and then did not stand up for him? What kind of sense can we make out of Jesus' mission?

These are all-important questions and we will return to them shortly. For the time being though, we must leave them to one side in order to bring out the nature of the resurrection as presented in the Scriptures. Jesus' resurrection is the second, inseparable element of the paschal mystery that does not end with death but that begins a strange temporal situation for Christ. On the one hand, when Christ appears bodily to his disciples, talks to them, and even eats with them, there is still something perceptible in this resurrection-time; while on the other hand, the relation to time is governed by different laws, since Christ appears and disappears, before he passes from the scene completely. If the risen Christ is truly human, time takes on a double form: that of our sense of duration that we can think of as meaningful, and that of Christ's sense of duration when this meaning is fulfilled. The connection between the two meanings is found in Jesus' word to his disciples: "And behold, I am with you always, until the end of the age" (Matt 28:20). Actual time, then, is "accompanied time," time that for those who believe the word of Christ takes on a coloration of "waiting": he will return.

THE END-TIME

If matters are as I have claimed, we can understand why Christian reflection is connected with the end-time, even though this specific moment eludes our grasp and can only be given a symbolic significance despite its continuity with our sense of real time. Whether on the level of the scientific philosophy of history or history that seeks to understand the succession of identifiable civilizations, the question of ultimate meaning cannot be avoided. When we try to understand this present moment in time, the question of the meaning of the whole of time spontaneously emerges. This is the perspective in which we must situate those writings we call "apocalypses" (see glossary), even if we must interpret their frightening aspects differently from how they were understood in times past.

Given a world today that is so familiar with terrors, there should be little wonder that apocalyptic thought has made such an impressive return. Such perspectives reemerge in times of crisis, and our age is certainly one of those. Christianity does not deny a certain element of catastrophe connected with the end-time, but this is not its ultimate meaning. Rather, meaning is found in our final relation to God, which is expressed in many scriptural texts. Take, for example, the following passage: "Thus we shall always be with the Lord. Therefore, console one another with these words" (1 Thess 4:17-18). The end-time will not be the removal of all duration, since duration is connatural to existence, but its transfiguration into total communication of God with humans and of humans with each other, in a world that has finally been reconciled.

ANTHROPOLOGY

Tragedy, Love, and Death

In order to better understand this perspective regarding the end-time and in order to see how it is realized in the death and resurrection of Jesus, we must consider death in more detail. We will try to understand it in relation to the more general human experience of *renunciation*.

If we define the human being as a creature that has many relations—with nature, with other human beings in all the areas of collaboration and friendship, and finally with God—we notice that none of these relations can be lived or attain true accomplishment without some renunciation or effort to transcend oneself, and that these are only possible in love. The discovery and the implementation of the relation of humans to nature implies preferences and choices, efforts and struggle, for it is not our nature as humans to find what we are in search of, except by a long and sometimes arduous process. To work with nature implies both imagination and respect. As the proverb says, by obeying nature one commands it. A certain "love" of nature must govern the process of investigating, producing, and consuming. At the very heart of our actual aspirations regarding ecology or bioethics is the sentiment and the experience that left to themselves, power and reason can obtain certain technologically impressive results, but at the expense of a general balance that is globally speaking more important. Our research must take the measure of our technical ambitions and exercise control over them. Here, as in other areas, reason must be allowed to lead by "love," to consent to limiting its activity. Though good and valuable enough in itself, in principle technology is in need of being subject to higher criteria of judgment.

Likewise, the relation of man to woman or man to humanity implies knowing and respecting the other and the imagination to recover ways of living that lead to the development of both parties. Ethics, if the word means the art of establishing just relationships among human beings, is based on a delicate interplay of recognition of the other and self-affirmation, or in other words, of knowing exactly how to work out the relationship between identity and difference. In this domain more than in that of nature, "love" and "death" encounter each other. A kind of dying to oneself is inevitable if the other is to exist, a dying that one gives consent to if the other's life is to have any worth in our eyes. This process is played out essentially on the level of an exchange of listening and speaking.[1] To listen is to be disposed to respond to all the bothersome accommodations that words introduce in my life. It gives consent to alterity. Its fruit is the emerging of a "we" where formerly there was only an "I" and a "he" or "she." Listening makes communion and collaboration possible. In other words, the human being cannot grow except by means of a transcending of oneself and one's horizons, a transcending that is beneficial and death-dealing at the same time.

The same norms govern the relation of men and women to God. According to Judeo-Christian revelation, the relationship is based entirely on listening to God's word and in loving obedience to the commandments. On the part of God who speaks, it is this mysterious "eccentric movement" beyond Godself in order to address human beings and to encourage their freedom. On the part of men and women, it is a going forth from themselves in order to learn about God and obey the word

---

[1] The primacy of language in interpersonal relationships is perhaps the most important finding of critical modernity, even if it is sometimes the subject of suspicion.

God addresses to them. We might note here that in the Bible, God's revelation is always connected to the challenge to a change of geographical place: the migration of Abraham, the Exodus, the Exile, as if it is not possible to know God by remaining where one is comfortably at home. The love of God and God's word sends the people and the individual ceaselessly forth, if the relationship is to grow deeper.

The result of this brief analysis is that we can call "death" the condition of establishing a relationship, whatever it might be. When spiritual beings are the subjects, the relationship is reciprocal, the result of giving, of waiting, and of welcoming. It includes its own "resurrection." Instead of having life out of myself, I have life out of the other, and this is an unending process. It is the happiness of love in action, the experience that everyone has sometime or other, even if it is brief.

What is constant in the three configurations that we have just considered—humanity to nature, one human being to another human being, and humanity to God—is a love that can be called "ecstatic." We must take leave of ourselves in order to approach the other and all the more so in order to welcome the other. The more spiritual the encounter with the other, the more complete the ecstasy. By that, Christian faith means that "God is love." Of course, God is infinite being (and we will have more to say about this point later), but only insofar as God totally gives away the divine being within Godself. Here is the most profound justification for the Trinitarian faith, a faith that confesses that the "Infinite" is "Exchange." Moreover, not only is God "Self-Exchange," but God has willed a communication outside Godself (if one is permitted to speak in this way). This communication can only be the offer of a covenant such that what exists between God and humanity will be the realization of what already exists in God.[2]

"Tragic Misfortune": Human Failure

Time is duration qualified by human freedom. It develops in the normal areas of work and fecundity, city life and peace, and all the other dimensions of human life, but as permeated at each moment by a relationship to God and founded on a divine word that is both demand and promise. In other words, the stages of time beginning with creation are those of relationship with God based on listening to God's word, having confidence

---

[2] In a certain way, what has just been proposed recognizes a point of contact between St. Bonaventure's *excessus amoris* ("superabundant love") and Hegel's dialectical schema or framework of reason.

in it and obeying it, and on the relationship of man to woman and ultimately of humanity to nature. These relations are correlative. From the
first pages, the Bible teaches that, should it happen, an event of rupture
in the relationship with God entails discontinuity in other relations. In
the space where humans encounter God and work the land, evil and violence, too, result essentially from the separation from God. Conversely,
faithfulness to God is the progressive restoration of peace and return to
the order of creation. An ensemble of negative relations that bear the
names idolatry, violence, and destruction is juxtaposed to an ensemble
of positive relations, tied to obediently listening to the word of God and
creating human and cosmic harmony. These three negative relations are
intimately connected to individual or collective self-affirmation that bring
with them certain advantages or entice us with certain pleasures.

Death is not only glorious, involving the renunciation of self in order to
welcome the other, but it is also an image of destructiveness and violence.
The game of "whoever loses, wins" is reversed: whoever wants to win at
life must lose. He or she forgets the covenant with God (idolatry), opposes
other human beings (violence), and destroys the cosmos (exploitation). This
self-affirmation is not without effects. In the short run, it unleashes its might
and garners pleasures, but tragic misfortunes are revealed after a while.
From its very beginnings, humanity has tasted this bitter experience, and
it is not a question of succumbing to pessimism if one says that evil grows
hand in hand with the false successes of reason acting without love.

Ultimately, time is bound up with a succession of double ruptures that
appear again and again. The one rupture arises out of the word of God
as demand and promise, and it is resolved in a constructive transcending
receptive to faith. Earlier, I called this rupture "tragedy." The rupture
that is bound up with sin, that is, with the refusal of the demand and
the spurning of the promise, I called "tragic misfortune." Sin not only
destroys the relationship with God but equilibrium among humans,
while the word of God constantly beckons humankind to listen to it as
it imparts meaning to whatever is destroyed by humans' refusal of God,
all the while turning to advantage what has been done, even unjustly. In
this way, the positive meaning of the human adventure is revealed only
against the backdrop of its contrary, evil as human refusal and cosmic
catastrophe. Discovering truth and consenting to evil walk side by side,
even if they are opposed, up to the day that marks the end-time. That
day will be both luminous revelation of meaning and the final onslaught
of absurdity. It will be the perfection of love and the full measure of evil.
But the latter will be reabsorbed into the former.

CHRIST

The Death and Resurrection of Christ: Tragedy

If we apply our reflections on time, love, and failure to the death and resurrection of Christ, we can come to a better understanding of what took place in his lifetime and ministry.

The abandonment by God that Jesus experienced is the ordeal that tests his love and faith, the act of transcendence we observed above that all the servants of God are invited to submit to: Abraham on Mount Moriah (Gen 22), Moses at the very entrance to Palestine (Num 20), Elias at Horeb (1 Kgs 19), and Jeremiah throughout his lifetime (Jer 15:10; 20:7). These individuals were subjected to a similar ordeal that paradoxically initiated them to the very heart of their prophetic mission. It is the same for Job and the Suffering Servant of Isaiah 53, non-historical biblical figures whose suffering opened the way to their unpredictable God. These servants of God discover that the ordeal is in reality a call to a relationship with God who meets them at the center of their being. The prophetic messenger brings his mission to completion when the servant of God paradoxically is elevated beyond his calling and his mission, attaining a covenant with God that is entirely personal. In their mission to men and women, everything becomes possible to those who reach such a degree of freedom.

The same was true of Christ, but his resurrection signifies that in him the process just described has reached its perfection. He who on the cross could say to God, "My Father," signifying that the ultimate meaning of "death" is the self-less invocation of God by humanity, understands that the words "My Son" spoken at the resurrection manifest the ultimate meaning of this event to be the pure invocation of humanity by God. At this moment, the "admirable exchange" between God and humanity that is the very heart of Christian revelation and the matrix of all Christian reflection achieves perfection. The suffering of the Just One (see Acts 3:14) and his liberation, the cross of Christ and his resurrection, are the authentic images of the very reality of God who is Gift and Exchange and who cannot do anything but call humankind to participate in his own Self. In the course of the church's history, those whom we call "saints"[3] lived and manifested this paradox of abandonment, death, and freedom.

Starting with this fundamental experience, the tragic inspiration of Christian reflection could be developed. An effort was made to speak

---

[3] The vocation to holiness is identical for all men and women. It is not limited only to those whom we call "saints."

about the paschal mystery with the help of words borrowed from the culture which had only negative terms to express the reality of love. Earlier, I used the expression "constitutive rupture." From St. Francis of Assisi to St. Theresa of the Child Jesus, it was just this experience of such a rupture that was at issue. In a film from the 1990s, "Francesco" by Liliana Cavani, the director showed forcefully that Francis, devastated by the failure of his effort to advocate absolute poverty in the following of Christ that he believed he had rightly received from God, finds peace not in some explanation of poverty, but in the gift of the stigmata of Christ's Passion. The ordeal of the faith for Theresa of Lisieux, or the existential questioning of all she had based her life on, did not abandon her during the last two painful years of her life. Without any weakening in her conviction, she submitted to the trial with the help of the blind constancy of her love. The radiance that was seen on her face after her death was the brilliance of the resurrection in one who had followed Christ in his Passion.

The Impact of Human Failure and the Nature of Redemption: "Tragic Misfortune"

From these perspectives, the final reason for suffering is not human failure but love. Nevertheless, the experience of failure concretely defines the context in which the suffering of love comes to us. In the perspective I am trying to present here, failure is not first transgressing the law, but the refusal of covenant and the rejection of the other. Perhaps better put, it is the refusal of the law, not as something defined that must be implemented, but as the intervention or claim of the other who offers his or her love by transcending all the reference points we have come to rely on. Again, such a refusal bursts in on us at all the levels of our existence and makes it difficult for us to have just relations with our peers and with nature. Violence against God leads to generalized violence. This means not only a rupture in relationships but destruction visited on reality. Death ceases to be the symbol and the place of love, and becomes senseless brokenness.

All of what I have described has no remedy, since humankind is not in a position to restore a relationship that has been broken and to reestablish the social and cosmic balance that has been destroyed. Such fractures and destruction bear in themselves the imbalances that can only be accentuated, so that, in our world of relationships and objective realities, there is really something like an instinct and a history of damnation. Doubtless, that is what classical theology means to express with the complex manifold of events it refers to as "Original Sin," and which recently Pope John Paul II (1978–2005) called the "structures of sin."

In this perspective, "redemption" can only come from God and consists of forgiveness that comes anew in the offer of covenant. The Bible is the history of this divine perseverance to "again and again present" Godself, always at the price of the fundamental transcending I spoke of. It is also the history of the reaction of love and hatred by human beings, letting reconciliation grow when they accept the offer, augmenting the violence and destruction when they reject it. Will there ever be someone who will respond to God's persevering love without reservation? Yes. Such a response was given by Christ on the cross which has left his body scarred by the physical, social, and cosmic violence of human failure. In this situation of "tragic misfortune," Jesus perseveres in invoking God and in the pardon given to men and women. He transforms the "tragic misfortune" of destruction into the tragedy of love. His resurrection shows that his response was perfect. Not only did he emerge victorious over the ordeal, but he resealed the covenant between God and humankind. Henceforth, no matter how great evil might grow to be, it can no longer be the equal of good, let alone surpass it. From this time forward, access to God is always possible in Christ, and that implies two elements that appear contradictory. First, to accept the "tragic misfortune" of the world with Christ—what the German theologian Dietrich Bonhoeffer (1906–1945) calls "watching with Christ in the Garden of Gethsemane." Second, to work for the restoration of the human and cosmic orders in all their forms. In the end, what will arrive, even if we do not know when exactly, will be global reconciliation, transfiguration, and love.

God

I want now to develop in greater detail what we can say about God from the perspective of desire, tragedy, and "tragic misfortune." Everything said above avails us the instruments we need to understand the gift, as it is lived in God. Christ reveals a total obedience to the word of his Father who sends him. Starting with the situation of brokenness in the world and among human beings, he offers himself to the One who sends him in the eternal Spirit and in the name of all of us (see Heb 9:14). The Father responds to this obedience by communicating to the Son incarnate, who has given himself in sacrifice, the fullness of life he is capable of receiving, both for himself and for all humankind. In the space that is called the "economy of salvation" (see glossary), we see the full manifestation of love.[4]

We believe that God *is* love. The property of love in God is without limits. In the human economy of the gift, we find a certain "quantity" that cannot be given. Concretely, to be human means being constituted a person in a defined and incommunicable way. It is possible that I can give everything I have, but not this personhood (unless I am called upon to physically sacrifice my life, but in this case I forever exclude it from an earthly exchange for love). This personhood is signified by my proper name and is the sign of my finitude. But it is the opposite with God. God does not need to protect some sphere or other of the divine from disappearing which would mean his annihilation. "To be God" does not mean to act in such a way as to be beyond giving and then to permit giving. "To be God" does not exist in advance of receiving the gift. "To be God" is always already found in the act of giving. If God is Reception, then God receives absolutely. If God is redemption, then God is such totally. Trinitarian love means that each person exists in an eternal movement of complete self-dispossession, but such that each is "compensated" by the equivalent gift of the other.[5]

It should be evident that the preceding proposition implies a careful analysis of our language when applied to God. We are equipped to speak about finite beings whose actions are circumscribed. And so, we express ourselves with finite concepts and words, even when we try to express the very limits of human possibility. Our words are bound to the experience of time, in other words, to moments "before" and "after" that are connected to each other by memory. Consequently, to speak the truth about love in God, we must take care not to transpose situations

[4] See "Trinity: Economic and Immanent" in A Glossary of Terms [translator].

[5] The Trinity is the deepest of life-giving mysteries, sustaining humanity precisely as mystery. In classical Trinitarian thought, theologians have developed a number of ways of conceiving and expressing this inner-trinitarian life. One of the most important ways has been to speak of a *"perichoresis"* or *"circumincessio"* among the "persons" Father, Son, and Spirit. In this passage, Lafont has been trying to show that another way of looking at the inner-trinitarian life is by way of the experience of gift. What is a gift in the final analysis? Is not our human experience of giving and receiving grounded in a giving and receiving that takes place primordially in God's own life? See "Trinity: Economic and Immanent" in A Glossary of Terms [translator].

too hastily, and in a way that would make the same claim to meaning in language about the mystery of Christ and language about the mystery of God.[6] If the transposition is to be considered and significant, it presupposes the mediation of the scriptural terms we employ to speak of the relationship of the Father to the Son in the Holy Spirit. They also demand a criticism that takes into account negative ideas, such as suffering and humility. They imply a careful study of the relationship between the name we use for *God* and the names we use to speak of *Father, Son, and Holy Spirit*. I propose now to speak about the first two points. I will examine the third point in the next chapter.

The Language of Revelation and Trinitarian Love

The range of words that reveal the mystery of the Trinity includes those that speak of *generation* ("the Son"), and that speak of the *word* (Word, Wisdom, *Verbum/Logos*), together with those that imply a certain dynamism of action ("force," "wind," "breath"). If the Father in God is only Father, or in other words, if there is no "before" to speak of regarding the subsistent and independent fatherhood of God, we can, and perhaps even *must*, think of the generation of the Son as a movement that is pure gift of the full divinity which the Father is and "empties out" on behalf of the Son. This "emptying out" is precisely what constitutes the Father as Father. Nevertheless, the Father is immediately "compensated" for this "emptying out" inasmuch as the Son in God "does not jealously cling to the divine form" (see Phil 2:6) he has received from the generation by the Father, but returns it totally at the very moment he receives it, in an act of thanksgiving that is as absolute in character as the movement of generation. The one "emptying out" corresponds to the other, and it is this act of total "restitution" that constitutes the Son as Son. The presence of the Spirit accounts for a third element in the double movement of generation (by the Father) and the act of thanksgiving (by the Son) by maintaining distance that allows for love (between Father and Son). It also signifies the happiness that results from the giving.

If the Son is also the "Word," we must try to consider the Trinity as *speech and response*. The means of doing this is the breathing forth of

---

[6] The technical term employed here by philosophers, and especially by logicians, is "univocity" or "univocal meaning." Terms and ideas that are exactly the same in meaning or scope are interchangeable. Lafont also warns us in this passage about the danger of falling into making a claim to univocity, even though we speak of the similarity as "analogous" or speak of "analogies" [translator].

the word. At the Word's origin is the one who is moved by the love of communication, and who addresses the situation by speaking. But in speaking, this one exhausts all that can be expressed. The "speaking" is the equal of "what is said," and the word is complete. The absolutely immediate response is also as complete as the speaking. The totality of the divine intelligibility is repeated by "the one who has been spoken" to "the one speaking."

Another way of considering the word is as *Law*, and Scripture gives us many examples. Every form of speech is an invitation to listen, and so, to make the change needed to open our ears and our hearts in order to be conformed to what we hear. Such listening is "obedience"—from the Latin *obaudire:* to listen intently—in the full sense of the word. The Trinity can also be contemplated from this perspective as commandment, obedience, and the breath of communion. This analogy is particularly vivid, because the gift, and so too the love, are tied to the Law. Whoever loves does the will of the one he or she loves, and so goes beyond one's own limited will. In human beings, obedience is the loss of some particular reality, something symbolic of an absolute gift, so that we might enter into full communication. We have seen how Christ carried such obedience to its limits. But in God, obedience has no limits.

I trust that these explanations are adequate for gaining some comprehension of the theme of God as Gift. It is a matter of stating that "God" does not exist as complete self-possession of the being that God is. God exists in communication that seems to be static, and that is the eternal movement of the "whoever loses, wins." If we want to say that God is love, we can claim that negative language is not bound up completely with the creature's finitude. Considered analogically, it speaks of pure perfection, love grasped in its infinite dynamism. Negative representation cannot be transcended, since it reveals the positive character of love.

Finally, at the level of the paschal mystery of Christ an element of *time* separates the gift (that is, the cross) from the response (that is, glory). There is no immediacy of the one to the other, at least on the level of human nature. This is not the case in God, however, where the gift and the response are absolutely contemporaneous, without the slightest distance separating them. Here is what the concept of eternity is all about, at least at the level of exchange in the Trinity.

The Limits of Talk about "Kenosis"

In this brief presentation, I have avoided speaking about "kenosis" in God, or in other words, completely transposing what the hymn in

Philippians 2:6-11 says regarding the mystery of Christ into an expression of the mystery of the Trinity. If what I have proposed in these pages is correct, humility and suffering come into play on two distinct levels: that of the tension between the movement of love and the inescapable finitude of existence, and that of the disjunctions born of the history of refusing love. The first level is that of tragedy, of trials, and of freedom; the second is that of the "tragic misfortune" that results from the refusal to obey. It can happen that "suffering" is transcended with a view toward the other, but such suffering is completely positive because it creates the possibility of exchange. Adam refused just this sort of "suffering," whereas Christ accepted it. Then there is suffering which results from turning in on oneself, so that I act against my desire for love. If one decides against all odds to love, a greater effort is needed to surmount this self-hardening which is not only personal but is nourished by all the refusals to love that have polluted history. Christ also bore the weight of this intensified suffering.

The word "kenosis" expresses well this double aspect of the mystery of Christ in his Incarnation and his paschal mystery. It implies the twofold overcoming of finitude and human failure. Now we cannot in any way posit such an act of self-surpassing in God. God is reciprocal Gift in God's very being and before all tragedy and all "tragic misfortune." God knows neither finitude nor guilt. God *is* love. If we cannot avoid using negative language to speak about this love, if the life, death, and resurrection of Jesus point out to us the way of correctly understanding the mystery of God as Gift, we must, I believe, carefully avoid anything that could nourish an anthropomorphic representation of God. The purity of the Gift that is internal to God is immune to everything in human beings that is negative. The purity of the Gift is love in all its joy.[7]

Brief Reflections on the Suffering of God

In making these observations, I am aware that I am taking my distance from a major theological movement in Trinitarian theology, one that

---

[7] Maurice Bellet's *Thérèse et l'illusion* (Paris: Desclée de Brouwer, 1998) has an expression for what I am trying to say: "The love Theresa believed she lived in her infancy, this perfect love without shadows: it is true, it is the ultimate truth of being human. I say again: love itself is without shadows. It might have to undergo many trials, many sufferings, and many separations—love suffers it. But in itself it is pure, without mixture. Love is only love" (p. 30). And God is only love.

follows Hegel and does not hesitate to speak of "kenosis" even in God, a kind of insertion of the cross in the Trinitarian relations themselves (the immanent Trinity). I also want to propose three parameters for evaluating language that speaks of God's suffering, without denying its eventual usefulness but also without employing it in a way that is too anthropomorphic.

The first parameter is *metaphysical*. Each thing suffers to the degree that it is. For example, we note that animals suffer, particularly animals that are more highly evolved. They are affected physically and psychically, but they do not possess language and their self-consciousness is elemental. We cannot imagine what suffering would be like that was not uttered or reflected upon. If this difficulty with perceiving what suffering among animals is like is a real one, then at the other end of reality, it would be difficult for us to imagine what suffering would be like for an angel or for God, both of whom are characterized by immateriality and whose reflective capacity exceeds our own. On the subject of suffering, as on all others, I think we must allow space for analogical meaning and take account of the distance between God and ourselves.

The second parameter is *moral*. I believe we cannot speak about the suffering of God before we have critically examined our own sufferings. These are profoundly qualified (or should I say, altered?) by the influence of our passions. Some we suffer objectively, physically, or psychologically, but others are characterized by an intensification of the suffering due to fear, resentment, anger, self-pity, and many other emotions. On this topic, it is important that we carefully check that the application of suffering to God does not proceed from a certain resentment we hold toward God. How is it that God can be perfectly happy while we suffer so much? How can a Father be so indifferent to the infinitely painful trials human beings are subject to? To be truthful, our understanding of the suffering of God must be as dispassionate as possible, and must guard against demanding an account of God. It must also carefully check its language when Scripture too speaks about the "passions" of God.

We can invoke the help of some early monks in whose minds the "battle against the passions" played a central role in asceticism and resulted in what they called *apatheia*, that is, a state of being entirely passion-free in a true state of internal freedom. *Apatheia* is also applicable in the areas of suffering and compassion. Ultimately, it is a matter of eradicating the sources of sufferings (*pathē*) that are not pure suffering. We understand, though admittedly somewhat confusedly, that a certain interior serenity (*apatheia*) needs to accompany true suffering and true compassion. At certain moments of grace, we have this experience of acute sensibility toward God, toward ourselves, and toward others, linked to an "unshakeable" interior peace. One doesn't permit its "destruction," or its "being shaken," by anything that transpires in us or around us. Now, far from making us unfeeling, such an interior state makes us closer to, or perhaps better said, more efficaciously open to a true consolation. It seems to me that in the light of such fleeting experiences of purity of heart in the midst of suffering we must try to think through the issue of God's suffering—though I admit we can do so only at great remove from the mystery of God.

For thirty years now, the notion of the "impassibility of God" has been under attack, and this attempt might correspond to a certain Stoic way of thinking. But shouldn't we look for an understanding of the impassibility of God more from the perspective of monastic experience? God is pure with respect to all passions, but that does not make God without feelings. We might imagine God's *apatheia* in terms of "tenderness"—on condition that reciprocally God's tenderness is thought of in a completely "passion-free" way, something that is almost impossible for us to imagine, but which we can try to understand. In short, I think we must "critique" our human experience of suffering before we start to apply it to God.

The third parameter is *theological*. If we say that God *is* Love and that God *is* Gift, then we must think of suffering within the very recesses of this "being-given." At this level, does the idea of suffering objectively add anything to the theme of God-as-Love? For us, doesn't love encompass in itself all that the theme of suffering conveys, if it is true that love is defined by the gift of life? For us who are "being" *and* "love," it is true that we have a need for rupture, change, "sacrifice," and "suffering" in order to transform our being into love. But if we try to think what love in God is like, in the perspective of total Trinitarian reciprocity, isn't the word "suffering" something illustrative *for us* of what is included in the absolute and exclusive reality of love in God? We should not think that divine love has nothing whatsoever to do with our tragedies and our tragic misfortunes. There is a greater measure of abnegation in the gift that is internal to God than in our limited gifts, even including our most tragic misfortunes, and even that gift of Jesus Christ as human. Nevertheless, divine abnegation is free of all the limitations that come with finitude and guilt, as well as with our human passions. Divine abnegation is infinite and reciprocal Gift. And so, the infinite intensity of the gift that is internal to God is of such a nature that the tragedy and the tragic misfortune of the mystery of humanity in Jesus Christ, and of all the vicissitudes of life's trials for humankind, find themselves reconciled as it were in the light of the gift that comes from God. If there were a total forgiveness of all offenses committed by men and women of all times, of all nations, and of all religions, this unheard-of pardon would still be a faint image of the love that is in God—of the Love that *is* God. Conversely, it is faith in this exemplary love that imparts the power to pardon, as we have seen in Jesus Christ.

CHURCH AND THE WORLD

Earlier, I recalled the definition of the church that is given in the chapter on the People of God of The Dogmatic Constitution on the Church, *Lumen gentium:* "The assembly of those who look to Jesus in faith as the author of salvation and the principle of unity and peace" (no. 9).[8] As theology is experienced in the churches today, this expression of faith is the memory of the cross and resurrection of Jesus and the lively awareness of the mystery of the Trinity. It is the modality by which the commandments of the Lord are presented and the committed response they elicit: "Hear, O Israel! The Lord our God is Lord alone! You shall love the Lord your God with all your heart, with all your soul, with all your mind, and with all your strength . . . [and] You shall love your neighbor as yourself" (Mark 12:29-30; cf. Luke 10:27). The liturgy is the place where the commandments are realized first and foremost, and the church is the first to observe them.

Liturgy

Christians find their points of reference by their symbolic practices. A person is baptized or not, goes or does not go to worship or to Mass, is married in church or only at the town hall, receives a Christian burial or not. These sacraments first of all participate in the religious foundation of all sacred signs that are related to life or death. Even in thoroughly secularized spaces, birth, marriage, and death are special moments attended by symbols that bring out their uniqueness. And there are other domains of life and death, such as seasons for planting and harvesting, departing for war and the signing of peace treaties. Implicitly, such rites signify that

[8] Norman P. Tanner, *Decrees of the Ecumenical Councils,* vol. 2 (Washington, DC: Georgetown University Press, 1990) 856.

these moments of human existence stand out because of special circumstances, precisely because they speak of the mysterious beginning of life, or of life's no less mysterious end. It is a matter of moments of rupture in the ordinary course of time, and that demands that their significance be pointed out. In religions, this particular dimension is tied to "another" world, that of our ancestors, of spirits, of deities, or finally of "God." Their meaning is signified by these rites, that is, gestures that have a human consistency about them. These include things like breath, speech, bathing, a meal, going on a journey, among many others, but whose celebratory context adds another signification, that of having a relation to hidden worlds where life has deep roots, namely, death and time.

If Christianity's source is the paschal mystery of the death and resurrection of Jesus Christ, by its symbolism and the words that express it, the Christian liturgy utters and makes present what I earlier called "accompanied time," when I made reference to the final verse of St. Matthew's Gospel where the risen Lord says: "I am with you always" (Matt 28:20). It brings to memory, that is, it arouses at the same time both recollection and hope. Humanly speaking, the Christian community and each of the faithful in particular live in the created duration that is theirs. But the ultimate meaning of this duration, fulfilled in Jesus Christ, is proposed to them in the rites that signify God's covenant and that appeal to their faith, and so provoke a "constitutive rupture" and invests the faithful with the power of the Spirit for living their lives in this time. It could be said that the "weak" rites found in secularized society are no more than passing interruptions in the course of time that continues to flow and is unchanged by them. The "strong" rites of a religious society on the contrary tend to uproot humans and their communities from time that merely drifts by and help them live with a view to "the other world." Between these two limits, and however precariously they are realized, Christian sacraments evoke and make present the end-time that has been fulfilled in Jesus Christ. They move toward the past, that is, the memory of what was accomplished "in those days," and toward the future anticipation of what will be made manifest. Thereby, the sacraments liberate this time by offering it a meaning that helps it unfold in truth. As I have said before, it is a time composed of "constitutive ruptures" and human accomplishments and sufferings that are no longer devoid of meaning.

Ethics

How does one live concretely in this time determined by the remembrance of the death and resurrection of Jesus Christ and celebrated and evoked in the sacraments? Thanks to the Spirit, we do this by applying the two commandments that encompass the whole law, as we saw above in recalling Jesus' teaching. As for the love of God, this is the domain of prayer. We listen intently to the word of God and respond with a heart that surrenders itself to God. Prayer entails an interiority, then, that knows it necessarily includes stages of tragedy and tragic misfortune, but also that it opens out more and more into silence and indescribable communion with God. As for the love of neighbor, let us note that it is common to the church and to the world of human beings. In the church, it is shared meditation concerning what one believes and whose truth never ceases to come again and again. It is also service and charity in the community, thanks to the discernment in common of what needs to be done or supported. Finally, it is mission, or offering the faith that makes us alive to those who are searching and whose quest we strive to understand. In the world, today often divested of any Christian reference, the second commandment is realized in what is called concern for the common good, and whose pursuit constantly demands the interplay of affirmation and denial I spoke of earlier when I pointed to its various levels, that of self and of various communities such as the local, regional, national, and international community. In the church, as well as in the world, this search for the common good is a true way of the cross, inasmuch as it incessantly demands that we attend to society's tragic misfortunes and wounds and respond to them. But it is also a way of love. This is what we call "ethics."

The first law of ethics is the law of the other. That means listening to the other's words and attending to his or her very being. Now such listening is both life and death. The objective contents of moral conduct, which I will say more about below, are inscribed in such a primacy of communion. Let us begin by expressing this in Christian terms. It is the mysticism of service that animates the Christian, a disciple of the "Servant of the Lord," or again what is referred to today as "the option for the poor" and which corresponds to the first beatitude of the gospel.[9] The poor person is like a sign of what Christian salvation is: because he has nothing, he can receive everything, and one can lose oneself in order to give to him. But if he is truly poor, he does not keep even the little he has received but offers it to another, and one can gain oneself back in

---

[9] "Blessed are you who are poor, for the kingdom of God is yours" in the version from the Gospel of Luke (6:20).

welcoming the gift of the poor person. Finally, the ethics of love is the ethics of the Beatitudes. Such an ethics of communion and of covenant is not condemned to the "self." To observe the commandment of Christ, it is also necessary to love oneself, otherwise how can one love the other "as oneself"? Everything depends on identifying the "self" and this might be the place to quote an expression of Paul Ricoeur (1913–2005). The French philosopher discussed the theme of "oneself as another,"[10] but I would like to modify it by speaking of "oneself as a poor person." Or one might also quote Georges Bernanos (1888–1948): "It is easier than one believes to hate oneself. The grace is to forget oneself. But if all arrogance were dead in us, the grace of graces would be to love oneself humbly like any other suffering member of Jesus Christ."[11]

However, in the task of putting the Beatitudes into action, there is not only the need for love as listening to the law and to the other, there is also the suffering of redemption, that is, the love that clears its path atop the ruins of humanity. This has always been admitted in the case of individuals. In today's context, which is that of advancing toward globalization, the way of redemption also manifests collective and cosmic aspects. These include the international community and planetary space, both of which bear the bitter fruits of human failure. In this context, the mysticism of service and the preferential option for the poor take on a frightful aspect of engagement. If we get to the bottom of things, it is not a matter only of turning one's attention to the poor, of practicing the works of mercy *for* them, in order to correct as many of the injustices created by the tragic misfortune of human failure as possible. The example of Christ who "became poor" (2 Cor 8:9) demonstrates that it is a question of being *with* the poor, and of discerning the situation *with* them and discovering both the evangelical and the political means to deal with it.

Without a doubt, here we have the point of departure of the "theology of liberation" that is hard to contest and that the bishops who have practiced it, and sometimes even died as a result (such as Bishop Oscar A. Romero [1917–1980]), say originates with the poor. It does not bring to the poor any light that comes from elsewhere. With discernment and avoiding complacency and demagoguery, it recognizes the light of the gospel

[10] See Ricoeur's *Oneself as Another,* trans. Kathleen Blamey (Chicago: University of Chicago Press, 1992), especially the chapter entitled "The Self and the Moral Norm," pp. 203–39 [translator].

[11] *The Diary of a Country Priest,* tr. Pamela Morris (New York: Macmillan Co., 1937; reprint edition, New York: Carroll & Graff, 1983).

present in the tragic misfortune of the suffering. In this context, it is hard to avoid certain Marxist analyses concerning the tragic mechanisms of the economy. There is also no reason for ignoring them, but just as happened formerly with the incorporation of ideas from Plato and Aristotle, there is an urgency today to move toward a critical discernment that is inspired by the gospel and serves it. In all honesty, once again we are just starting to come to terms with the primacy of the poor. Nevertheless, we sense that if there must be such a thing as "globalization," as there was such a thing as "Christendom" at the end of the Middle Ages, it can be constructed in a way that avoids tragic misfortune only if it starts with the poor.

In the context of the tragic misfortune that characterizes the world today, the preferential option for the poor inevitably takes on a political dimension, if only because it must define the fundamental principle of politics in a troubled world, and do so even without any Christian reference points. To start with the poor is the best means of assuring the common good, so that no single person is excluded. Christians are also citizens and they have the duty of exercising vigilance over what their faith community bears in mind and the duty of helping put into practice, as much as possible, the fundamental principle of the common good today. Naturally, such a concern by Christians can create conflicts. But are we not dealing here with a particular application of a model at the same time necessary and unstable? The state and religion are distinct but not separate, and they never were. As the history of the church amply shows, the state and church share borders and their relations are often in conflict. Though the contexts were different, popes and emperors did not shy away from confronting one another. The alliance of throne and altar always had its shadow side and rivalries, and the separation of church and state was often experienced as hostility to each other. Moreover, even when relations were more friendly or diplomatic, they risked becoming insignificant in real life, at least when they showed a weakening of the church's resolve to proclaim the gospel precisely in those situations where sin trampled underfoot the dignity of men and women. Today, in most countries, the churches no longer have political standing and are not in the position to offer a final, authoritative word. Nonetheless, they have not given up the attempt to teach with authority, even if their message is often not listened to. Those churches are fortunate when the words they speak correspond to their actions. We thank God there are situations where an authoritative word of teaching is received by the faithful and their pastors who are prepared to die for the word of the gospel, a word that speaks the truth about human existence.

CONCLUSION

We conclude our treatment on time and covenant by remarking that it has attempted to give a "modern" expression to how tradition regarding Christ, God, and human beings can be presented today. We emphasized how, since the high Middle Ages in the West, the humanity of Christ appeared in the light of his loving Passion suffered for humankind. Among others, the name of St. Bonaventure was cited. Then came Luther, who perhaps over and above his Augustinian background and inspiration, rediscovered the force of St. Paul's intuition, "[Christ] has loved me and given himself up for me" (Gal 2:20). In other words, salvation has been given in Jesus Christ, it is powerful, and it belongs to the one to whom we must constantly entrust ourselves if we are to live without anguish and in unending hope of our salvation. This is the message taken up again in our day by St. Theresa of the Child Jesus, with an insistence on love that was never equaled in the past. Undoubtedly, the grace of our time is to have seen that this manifestation of merciful love in the past millennium confesses not only God's attitude vis-à-vis us but unveils the pure love that is in God and reveals the mystery of the Trinity in a new and different way. It has also meant the discovery anew of the collective dimension of salvation: tragedy and tragic misfortune are intertwined and resolved at the level of Christian and human communities. The nuance that I have tried to bring out here, in distinguishing tragedy from tragic misfortune, aims at creating even greater distance from the specter of sin. In no way is sin to be found in God, not even alongside God, whereas in man it finds its true definition: offense against the one who loves. Thus, in the light of forgiveness that not only forgets evil but reintegrates humankind in the truth, everything that comes under the suffering of tragic misfortune can become the way of humanity and its divinization.

Chapter Six

CREATION AND BEING

We have just completed the great topics of theology, namely, anthropology, Christ, the Holy Trinity, the church and the world, from the perspective of the dialectical understanding of history whose guiding norm is the paschal mystery of Jesus. In order to avoid the erroneous conclusion that evil and sin are not included as "necessary" elements of the dialectic, I introduced the distinction between "tragedy" (*la tragédie*) and "tragic misfortune" (*le drame*), and I showed how suffering must be disentangled from evil in order to be correctly understood. We saw that this is what Scripture does, especially the book of Job.

Nevertheless, it seems that we have not yet said everything. We confess that the Father, the Son, and the Holy Spirit are "one only God." Often in theological contexts, the word "God" is employed without spelling out further whether it is a matter of one divine person, of all the divine persons, or which divine person is being referred to. What signification can we give to the designation "monotheistic" that we share in common with Judaism and Islam? Likewise, the church and Scripture speak of Jesus in terms not only of the paschal mystery but of the Incarnation, that is, his identity as the Word incarnate. What is to be said about these matters?

Concerning anthropology, we have spoken about tragedy as a conflict between different desires, good in themselves but that must agree to a certain renunciation in order to build a "we." But what is a "good" desire? What accounts for the goodness of a desire and what are the criteria for consenting to a transcending of desire, bound as the consent is to the word of the other that fulfills and does not destroy the good desire, even under the pretext of altruism? Furthermore, two or more individuals can conspire to do evil. In this case, their consent does not suffice for defining what is good. In terms of ethics, if the primary law is the "law of the other," is it possible to verify, however minimally, that such a law is "legitimate" and not arbitrary, and therefore should be obeyed?

And so, in theology as in anthropology, we are faced with language that has been antecedently determined. It does not function well in the context of the language of "constitutive rupture," dialectic, history, and love. We need to develop better explanations based on the notions of "the One," "being," "person," the commandments, and others. We need to develop understandable contents that are relevant to the multiformity of reason. If we recall the historical outline sketched out earlier, we see that ancient theology favored just such language of "the One," "being," "person," and commandments. But today, must we recognize a similar theological space, make room for it, and articulate it to others?

Already modernity itself invites us to consider the task as necessary. The very idea of dialectic presupposes that an outmoded term is later recovered and transformed in the developmental phase that follows it. Thus, ancient and medieval theology must resurface in some form in modern theology. History forgets nothing, but integrates everything. In the case before us, we must examine how this integration comes about. Then, it is on the level of reason that matters are being worked out and have been worked out in large part regarding the question of modernity.

As we have seen, modernity signifies the emergence of human beings from a mythological world that was more or less bound to imagination. Furthermore, it signifies access to the real as knowable and of utility to men and women. It also includes the possibility that humans determine the conditions of their actions. If the excessively mathematical aspect of the modern use of reason (*mos mathematicum*) has caused certain philosophers today to reject it, we still have the right to call for its restoration in a larger horizon of reason. Whatever philosophers and theologians think of the matter, the reason of modernity still operates among scientists, technicians, and ordinary people in their day-to-day activities. We must, then, rethink it.

This chapter will evaluate the possibility of reason and understanding in the work of theology. To keep the point of departure as simple as possible, I will begin where the last chapter left off—with ethics. Then, little by little, I will hazard making some proposals regarding the idea of metaphysics, the concept of creation, and finally the possibility and advantage for dogmatics, or systematic theology. I will conclude on the possible articulation of language that is static, rational, and intellectual, with language that is dynamic, temporal, historical, and covenantal.

ETHICS

We saw that the "law of the other" is the fundamental moral principle. It is underscored and accentuated by the two commandments of the gospel and the Beatitudes. Experience proves, however, that for it to bear fruit, the gift of self must be reflected on. If the gift that has brought life for the other is to remain an ultimate light for guiding our conduct—and here it is the death of Christ, but of many others also, that has given us an example—at least as long as our life is not threatened, it is necessary to accept less than total modes of giving. Only a process of discernment in which sensibility and reason play their irreplaceable roles can permit us to truly give ourselves without destroying ourselves. In the vocabulary I have suggested, we can say that it is a matter of determining in life's ordinary circumstances the conditions of a true "tragedy." But that presupposes some *analyses*. But what will be the criteria governing them? In other words, how can we make more precise the right measure of the gift?

Let us return for a moment to history. We alluded earlier to the "Spiritual Franciscans," those passionate devotees of poverty who so lived in the image of the crucified Christ that they could not tolerate the idea of owning anything in the world, not even the most insignificant possession. This extreme position signifies their refusal of the human condition, in view of a life lived in eschatological anticipation of the end-time. It implies the rejection in principle of all reflection on the basic needs of human nature. And even if they must concede a minimum of this world's goods in order to be able to live, think, love, and finally to be connected to God in truth, they do not try to ground this minimum requirement in reason. I spoke further about nominalism that only knows the singularity of the individual facing a world of possibilities and excludes the definition of a universal human nature that would help orient human action, at least in broad strokes. It seems to me that in these two cases (and they are after all still contemporary), primacy is given to a dynamism that knows no boundaries. There is the "vertical" movement toward God by way of the absolute poverty of Christ and genuine Christians; and there is the "horizontal" movement toward an infinite number of possibilities, in service of the unconditioned freedom of the singular individual. In these two cases, there is no immanent norm for helping resolve one's desires. Actually, such a pure love and such unlimited singularity are impossible for human beings as they really are. We must attribute to such actions that are found in time a minimum of motives that are morally qualified, that is, that channel desire so that it can bear fruit that is truly human. Is it really necessary to emphasize that today's bio-ethical controversies are all about this question? One senses today that notions like "freedom, the other, and the possible" are no longer sufficient for a complete determination of what is good for the individual human and humankind.

If this is the way things are, we cannot avoid inquiring about what can be called, in the widest sense of the term, the "constants" that must be defined, at the level of our psyches, our bodies, and our conduct. They play the role of points of reference along the way of individual freedom as well as for those exchanges that constitute unending human tragedy. If total nominalism, mystical or practical in form, is impossible for leading an ethical life, then we must admit the theoretical pertinence of words like "nature" and "essence" as ways of measuring and regulating desire, while trying to grasp them "in their nascent state" as it were, and without being laden with all the speculations they have been subjected to over the centuries. Such terms are available to us to signify that human freedom is in a way preceded by a general situation of the real and that this freedom can be exercised only by being oriented to this situation.

The difficulty is found in concretely discerning these constants, so that they can continue in the service of authentic freedom. We need to avoid using them in a way that would annul their efficacy, by putting them in a straightjacket, as it were. Concretely, we must find a balance between fundamentalism and liberalism. In its extreme form, fundamentalism consists of searching in the letter of Scripture or tradition for a rule or clear and tidy indication of what men and women must do. The constants are thought to be all the more "protected" if they are thought to have been established by God. The singularity of the individual or the novelty of a word spoken in exchange has no place here. It is simply a matter of applying the rule to the changing situation. Time and history play no role either, nor does reason. The moral norm, in effect, comes directly from the "One on high" and expresses not "divine reasons" for acting but the "will" of God. In a more refined form, fundamentalism is the once-and-for-all definition of "natural laws" and "divine laws," which have become more and more precise as the investigation unfolds in the course of time. The claim is made that such laws, because they are "natural," should be evident to everyone, and that eventually a religious authority could proclaim them to anyone who is ignorant of them. Here, in principle we find reason, but reason that is constrained and made ever-more precise in the sources of secular moral reflection, so that the imperative character of actions is more important than their reasonableness. Conversely, liberalism consists in reserving ethical decisions only to the individual freedom of men and women, in a kind of implicit confidence, which is continually belied by the facts, that some sort of equilibrium will eventually emerge and establish itself between persons and with regard to nature.

In reality, the genuine search for ethical conduct is written in a reflective tradition of a rational type in which human investigation has unearthed certain basic constants. In the case of Christianity, where the Word of God has handed on orientations, and where Christian communities have discovered ways of acting, and where there has been contact with ethical criteria other than solely Christian ones, understanding is expanded. But, as Christian reflection addresses problems that former stages of civilization had no consciousness of, it returns to ethics to find concrete reasoned answers to questions that are to some extent genuinely new. Dialogue and a spirit of renunciation are of help here, but on condition that they serve the building up of good ways of acting. Ethics is *discovery* and not the invention of a given order of reality. It is *discernment* because it is a matter of orienting a way of acting that is not totally in the power of freedom. But ethics is also *foundation*, since within its limits it pertains to human beings to construct the moral dimension of their action.

We can assert that ethics, under the guidance of moral contents, progresses in two senses. First of all, time is needed to discover the correct answers to problems that are ever new. Here is where human finitude enters the picture with its slow pace impeding the understanding of fundamental matters. Then, efficaciously moving from what is to be wished for to the possible takes a long time and is laborious. Here is where the weight of accumulated disorder comes in, a weight that one cannot be rid of in an instant. The perspective of redemption and hope can help us admit this twofold lethargy that ethics suffers from. But, slow-paced or fast, ethics founded on discernment is a matter of reasoned analysis that is possible only with the help of carefully distinguishing the diverse orders of reality.

To conclude, if we look for some unity in our observations relating to ethics, we can say that Christian reflection strives to deal with the paradox created by a twofold moral inspiration. There is an ethics of gift defined by love that accepts the loss of self and locates not only its model but also its source in the paschal mystery of Christ. But there is also an ethics of discernment defined by intelligence that searches the ways of authentic self-affirmation, helped by an order of reasons and situations. One also finds many examples in the admonitions of the biblical writings of the Old and New Testaments. Balance must be sought over and over again, both on the level of individual persons and of the community. The two inspirations contain an element that is not insignificant in the fight against the egoisms and rationalizations that are deeply inscribed in the psyche, but that one can subject to the force of authentic freedom.

METAPHYSICS

We think that what is needed to discern the truth of the "law of the other" in relationships that are interpersonal and more broadly political is the discovery of certain constants with objective contents. Starting from the domain of ethics, we are now justified in extending our reflection and implementing a careful and subtle consideration of "metaphysics," that is, a more general analysis at the levels of the real and the degrees of being and action from the perspectives of their coherence, their autonomy, and their pertinence to the human search for meaning.

It is true that recourse to metaphysics is contested today. The challenge is helpful to the extent that it forces us to refine the very concept of metaphysics. Two major objections can be raised. The first arises out of what is to be understood under the heading of "metaphysics," identified as it often is with "onto-theology." The latter is a rationalist type of thinking that claims that "everything that is real is rational," including God. Such a form of rationality arising out of modernity's *mos mathematicum,* and which I called "triumphant modernity," is to be rejected. But the same is true of the other form of modernity, the "dialectical," which seeks to encompass nature and history in an organic, encyclopedic, and flawless system, like the one Hegel tried to construct. If this was the only possible meaning of the word "metaphysics," one would be quite correct in rejecting it. But this is not necessarily the case.

As its name indicates, metaphysics does not pretend to encompass morals, anthropology, physics, or any other discipline, but it does attempt to reach a very fundamental level (*meta*) of thought and existence and to speak about it.[1] It tries to pinpoint the signification and the relevance of perceptions that are the most general and that underlie all our discourse and all our desires, whatever our philosophical or religiously confessional convictions may be, and that translate themselves into such words as "being," "oneness," "the good," and "the real." Metaphysics allows considerations like these, present but hidden, to rise to the level of thought. This is a task that is never finished and an effort of attentive knowledge, which is anything but the emergence of an autonomous rationality that seeks to understand reality exhaustively and to claim as much.

The second objection that is raised against metaphysics arises from its being incompatible with history, or more generally speaking, with change. In a scientific universe where one speaks about "relativity" (Albert Einstein [1879–1955]) and the "principle of indeterminacy" (Werner Heisenberg [1901–1976]), there seems to be no place anymore for words like "essence," "substance," and other such metaphysical terms. In a world marked by the constant and unexpected roles of tragedy and tragic misfortune, words like "order" and "stability" seem out of place. It is no longer possible today to understand what is real only in terms of what is speculative, or fixed, or above considerations of time and history. In centuries past and in places untouched by modernity this was not the case. And yet, the question still remains: what is the proper proportion of such constants as the meta-historical, the meta-numerical, and the meta-physical that is needed for our discourse and our scientific and historical theories to be of service?

To answer such a question, I want to hazard a reflection at this point on a model that is rather current today for thinking about the history of the cosmos, namely, the big bang theory. According to this theory, the very first moment that astrophysics points to neither had nor can have a properly rational designation. We use an image, that of a primordial explosion that is thought to be historical, and after which we can reconstruct a chronology of the universe's origins that is thought to be historical: three seconds after the explosion, sixty seconds, several minutes, and so forth. But such a chronology is recognized and qualified only by reason of the appearance of various *bodies* that are distinguished from one another and whose properties can be analyzed by attributing to them an influence in

---

[1] In Greek, the prefix *meta* in "metaphysics" can mean "below" or "beneath," hence "supporting," "grounding" or "prior to" [translator].

the subsequent history of the universe. Much, much later life will appear and then human beings, who in turn form the object of historico-rational study. Put another way, the temporality of the world can be enunciated in this model only due to the consideration of a diversity of beings who, even if they emerge from the same movement, do not for all that lack their own coherence. Constantly, there is *event*, but it generates a *structure*. We cannot make sense out of becoming without taking into account the formulas of being that offer sufficient constancy, so that we can seek to explain their stability. Without a doubt, delimiting and determining such constants is difficult and often uncertain. And still we find these constants, so why not use with discretion the philosophical word "essences" for them? It is possible that the model of the big bang will be abandoned in the future, in the light of other findings. But, whatever other model will someday be proposed, it seems unimaginable that it will not include a new and original articulation between *meaning* and *structure*. Meaning is the direction and the signification of some general dynamism, while structures are the supporting points that are indispensable for recognizing meaning, and from these latter it is possible to form a concept.

An idea that has currency in the philosophy of science and that can be of assistance here, is the notion of "weak objectivity." It brings out a specific aspect of knowledge, namely, that when we make an observation, the observer comes into play, so that a certain subjectivity must be included in the expression of the reality observed. Such a subjective factor of knowing also plays a role in the understanding of history. A statement that would ignore this subjective factor and would want to speak exclusively in absolute terms would be influenced by an assumedly "strong objectivity." But is such an objectivity possible? The scientist will resist the temptation and say instead: "A statement is said to be 'weakly objective' when it brings the notion of the observer into play, but claims that the observation is true no matter who the observer is."[2] The universality of what is claimed to be true points to a "hidden real" that supports the statement, without reason being able to grasp it. I wonder if this is not what, in the end, the word "to be" means. Is it not a word whose intelligible content is minimal, in terms of a definition, and that is still implied in every statement of a speculative or historical character? It's the same with metaphysical expressions in general. Their

---

[2] Bernard d'Espagnat, *Traité de physique et de philosophie* (Paris: Fayard, 2002) 111.

aim is the primary apprehensions and the universal and elementary statements that one can barely pose for oneself without posing them for others as well. Their usage is both constant and fragile. One might say, using other words, that the field of metaphysics is governed by a spirit of subtlety and not geometry. Perhaps we must relearn how to speak in a new, almost juvenile way the words without which there is no language. In the first place, that means the language of "being."[3]

CREATION

In order to shed some light on all these questions, Christian reflection employs the notion of *creation*. In the Bible, the word appears first of all in the context of history: "In the beginning, when God created the heavens and the earth" (Gen 1:1). It does not stop at the creative act inasmuch as it brings about the first instant and initiates the unfolding of time. It also attributes to God the limits of the various orders of reality, beginning with inanimate things right up to the human being, who is considered to be the image of God (see Gen 1:26). Highlighting the wisdom of God, the world is presented as a series of separations in the chaos of the cosmos.

---

[3] I want to point parenthetically to a delicate problem, and one for which I do not have the solution. Scientists seem to be in agreement that, at a certain level of preciseness in their theories and in practice, they need to place themselves in space as envisioned by relativity and quantum theory, but that, as far as physical measurements and interventions that are less specialized are concerned, Newtonian physics is perfectly adequate. If this is how matters stand, it is hard to refuse a certain degree of truth to Newtonian physics. It appears, then, that we must develop a theory of different languages of physics and of each language's relevance. Such a theory of different languages needs to be seen as a way of acknowledging that there are different levels of truth. One could ask if the question should not in fact be extended. For example, is Copernican cosmology a complete rejection of the cosmology of Aristotle and Ptolemy? The question arises out of the observation that even if we are completely convinced that the earth revolves around the sun, our eyesight seems to see the reverse. One might add many other occurrences where appearances, and not theory, control our use of language. Such incidents ground the symbols (see glossary) we use and furnish us with reference points in our practical lives. Is such an appearance completely devoid of truth? Rather, when we consider synthesizing the various levels of research and the statements that have been made from Aristotle up to Max Planck (1858–1947), isn't it necessary to try to formulate a general theory that is inclusive of the various languages used in physics, of their degrees of truth, and of the metaphysics that result from them?

The result is a harmonious symphony of various realms that nonetheless have a certain coherence and compatibility among them. Creation is not just about history but treats how reality can be intelligibly defined. Again we find the distinction between *meaning* and *structures* that underlay our discussion of the big bang, and that even seems to be a primitive model of human intelligence as capable of functioning at the level of myth (see glossary) or of reason. This vision found at the beginning of the Bible is taken up later in the works that are referred to as the Wisdom literature. In the line traced by revelation, Christian reflection believed it was authorized to scrutinize the various levels of reality, just as science and philosophy do. It was thought that every being is, in principle, open to an analysis that brings out its essence and its properties, even if great care must be taken in doing this.

Interest in the notion of creation is what gives realities—limited, subtle, measured in their capacity—a right to exist. "God saw how good the light was" (Gen 1:4).[4] If there is no creation, then all these things are in some way or other "superfluous." Since we do not know where they come from or what they are meant for, we attempt to devise a system that explains them but that ultimately results in their disappearance. When all is said and done, there remains only the great Everything—and for that reason it should really be called Nothing. The least improper word for speaking about the Everything/Nothing is "the One." Here, "the One" is a purely negative term that excludes all multiplicity and every imaginable property. Concerning "the One," it really has "no name or number," so that everything that is individuated and can be named would be destined to disappear. Finitude, then, is something evil. On the contrary, if there is creation, everything limited that exists has meaning and value. It has a proper name and a common name, and a number that marks off its dimensions. The name "being" in particular can be significant. Its logic is available by making its attribution more precise. Nothing is "superfluous" and the origin of evil is to be sought elsewhere, and not in finitude.

The Being of God

Speaking of God, can we take one more step and say that God *is*? If the use of the word "being" is necessary to establish the double claim

---

[4] The point is accentuated by the repetition of the phrase, "God saw how good it was," or some variant of it, in verses 10, 12, 18, 21, 25, and 31 [translator].

that God is in God's very self Gift—the Trinity as mutual exchange—*and* that God is creator, then there is no reason to shrink from using the word "to be" of God.[5] In trying to describe the gift in God in the preceding chapter, I wrote that "to be God" is always already in the Gift, that God does not exist apart from or before the gift. To say that in no way denies the fact that God "is," but it does affirm God as that which is and gives himself in exchange in such a way that each divine person does not stop at himself. It is the totality of Being-given that allows us to continue to claim the monotheism that is the very heart of our Trinitarian belief. Sometimes we speak of "Trinitarian monotheism," and what we want to say with this phrase is that God is not the One God if God is not Gift. To speak of God's oneness implies the being of God, and that is what the substantive "monotheism" is trying to express, while the adjective "Trinitarian" points in the direction of the Trinity of persons. The task of the theologian consists in responding to the apparent contradiction in the claim. That is what the councils up to St. Thomas Aquinas attempted to do by using the notions of "being" and "relations" in particular. If one chose to enunciate the traditional Trinitarian faith by using the unwonted expression "unitary tritheism"—an expression that is not current but could also be justified to underscore the Gift in God—it would be necessary to explain where the adjective "unitary" comes from. To fail to do this could open Christianity to the accusation of tritheism pure and simple (that is, Christians confess three gods), a claim the other two monotheistic religions, Judaism and Islam, have made. To counter the claim and explain the adjective, I do not see any other way but by speaking of the "being of God." We cannot speak of Gift by only considering the *action*—without being willing to say anything about *who* is given. That the gift is always given and returned at the same moment does not signify that it does not exist. If we attach the word "God" to the word "Father," as we do in the Creed ("I believe in God, the Father almighty"), or if we were to attribute it to each person, as we do in theological reflection after the Council of Nicaea (God the Father, God the Son, God the Holy Spirit), in any event the word "God" has a definite signification, and the word "being" seems

[5] In the sentence I have just written, the word *God* is subject of the verb "to be" twice. Theologians who are the most reticent to say that "God is," in the metaphysical sense, do not for all that hesitate in their presentations and their reasoning, to make God the frequent subject grammatically of a sentence where the verb "to be" is used. This phenomenon does not strike me as harmless, since language that is used often cannot be really without significance.

to be the word that best expresses it. It is at one and the same time the most indeterminate and the most extensive of nouns. It is the most indeterminate because it speaks only about pure existence, without adding any further precisions to it. It is the most extensive because no other word makes sense except by implying this very word (to be).

I suppose it appears to the reader that when one uses the word "being" apropos of God, we are very far indeed from the understanding of God as *causa sui* in modernity. There, as *causa sui,* God is an element that is intrinsic to the total rationality of what is real. The limit of all discussion of "theism" is found in the fact that it refers in a quasi-exclusive way to the God of modernity and to the supposed metaphysics that is bound up with it. Now that we are beyond seventeenth-century preoccupations, we must retrieve certain basic insights of ancient theology, in order to integrate them into more contemporary theological reflection on God. From this point of view, to confess God as creator helps us understand the divine name "Being," if it is true that what God communicates is a true though limited participation in what God is in plenitude. The idea of creation implies both the consistency and the autonomy of each creature (that which permits the creature also to enter freely into the economy of mutual exchange) and communicates an unbreakable relation to the creator. The word "being" (to be) determines a limit in the creature, whereas in God it aims to express what is infinite.

Naturally, attributing to God the name "Being" presupposes an analysis of the conditions of legitimate and significative attribution of this name. But this goes for each and every divine name. In fact, whether it pertains to God or to anything else for that matter, we speak in three registers: action (as with the Gift, for example), being, and relation. In the course of the centuries, the logic of these divine attributions has given rise to studies that might be described as fully deploying the linguistic resources available to them by using all the ranges of signification in language: concrete/abstract language, proper/appropriated language, real/notional language, and univocal/equivocal/analogical language, as well as the various combinations of these ranges in each scenario. Unfortunately, this type of work has fallen into disuse, and one finds very few contemporary theologians who are as careful as medieval theologians were in their logical qualification of propositions relating to God. It is to be hoped that the current renewal of logic in analytical philosophy, for example, will lead theology back to this highly neglected task.

A final comment concerning Christian dogmatic (or systematic) theology will now be appropriate. In the chapter dedicated to the theology of the era of the fathers of the church, I sketched out how the dogma of the Trinity was, as it were, born out of the necessity of speaking about the proper status of the mediation of Jesus Christ. Are not these questions making a return today, and almost in the same terms as in the past, to the extent that men and women in the West are now becoming aware of Oriental thought or Indo-European ideas, characterized by strong convictions of the attraction of oneness and the primacy of mysticism? The Indian formula known by the name of *advaita,* that is, the "One who has no second other," encounters the Trinitarian faith head-on. Isn't the problem today the same as in Christian antiquity, when it was the question of admitting the divine sonship of Jesus Christ, and then having the problem of resolving how to speak properly about his divinity, without for all that admitting the existence of a "second God," as was done in pagan circles? We do not yet know how to orient this reflection of Christian theology in dialogue with the mystical East. I can only indicate the existence of the problem and say that up to the present Christian reflection has not been able to find another way of thinking through the faith at the level of how we name God and Christ exactly. The only instrument known to us comes from metaphysics, a metaphysics considerably refined in terms of its sources and because of the demands that were made on it to speak of God.

The Sacraments

We have spoken about the Christian liturgy from the perspectives of time and covenant. The framework of creation and being also favor an understanding of the sacraments (see glossary) in terms of the efficacy of the mystery of Christ vis-à-vis humankind, and not simply in terms of how Christians specifically understand time. What these symbolic gestures signify concerning the economy of salvation, they also concretely realize for men and women by sealing them definitively with the image of Christ. They communicate grace, that is, our participation in the divine nature (see 2 Peter 1:4) and adoption as sons and daughters, which are the objective conditions of communion with God, the ultimate goal of all of salvation history. The body and blood of Christ who died and rose again are *really* present in the Eucharist and it is just this presence that makes it possible for the time of the resurrection and glory to erupt in our time. The sacraments of Christian initiation, baptism and confirmation, not only signify but also bring about an objective bond with the Word incarnate who died and rose again and with the Spirit of promise. In the liturgy of reconciliation, sins are *effectively* forgiven, indicating that re-creation is once again at work in men and women. In other words, Christian ritual, in the very act of symbolizing, transfers men and women into the space of the kingly rule of God without withdrawing them from this world. Because it is a matter of two different yet concomitant dimensions, it situates them paradoxically in the ultimate truth of time and being.

CONCLUSION

In the theological outline I have just sketched, I have used two languages, that of history (which is death and life) and that of being and creation. It is my conviction that we cannot reduce them simply to one language, certainly because of the inadequacy of our human words, but also because of the objective complexity of what we must speak about. Each of these two discourses is indispensable for the proper operation of the other, and there will be necessary compromises between them that will take various forms, depending on which language one chooses to give greater weight to.

A particularity of our presentation would reverse the order in which these two languages come to expression. In the section entitled "The Itinerary," speculative theological language came first in our discourse: from the term "consubstantial" declared at the Council of Nicaea to "transubstantiation" at the Council of Trent, we spoke in the linguistic range of being, substance, nature, order, and stability—even if in the cases of these two terms the root word *substance* was "broken" in order to suggest some philosophically improbable significations. In itself, *substance* precludes appending any prefix, since it intends to express the fundamental unity of the real. The prefixes "con" (*con*substantial) and "trans" (*trans*substantiation) introduce us by their very presence to another world of thought and being. The theological language of history, or more generally, of "motion," arrived with the astronomical, geographical, and scientific findings of the Age of Discovery. These findings necessitated a series of changes. First, it was necessary to think through the question of novelty because of its massive arrival in this period. Next, thinkers had to introduce the categories of memory and prediction into the mix of reason. Then came the introduction of subjectivity into the act of knowing and of rediscovering interpretation in the place of assertion alone. Finally, it was necessary to discover how the perception of development left its mark on the expressions of faith and how it relativized the pretension to supposedly definitive classical language.

In the section entitled "Theology in Outline," however, time and covenant were the first to arrive on the linguistic scene, followed by creation and being. Modernity, despite the distance it has often desired to put between itself and Christian revelation, points to a framework of thought that corresponds best with this revelation. The final redactor of the Scriptures ordered them in such a way that they are divided between the book of Genesis ("In the beginning") and Revelation which offers insight into "the end-time." Salvation is not principally a matter of reflection but of history. It is concerned with our awareness of the divine purpose always already decreed, of getting on with what is in progress in faith, hope, and love, and of hastening the moment (*kairos*) of the Savior's coming. Moreover, the dynamism of history, with its modalities of tragedy and tragic misfortune, is shown to be capable of manifesting the very essence of revelation, namely, the mystery of the death and resurrection of Christ and the intimate life, in the form of gift, of the Father, the Son, and the Holy Spirit. I will suggest a bit later that this form of thinking, which corresponds moreover to the state of Western culture today, is of its very nature meant to order the human spirit toward an authentic globalization, not an oppressive one. It values the primacy of communion as the expression of the reality of love and the dignity of human beings who are the subjects and agents of this communion.

Reflection on creation, posited as both an act of God and the autonomous consistency of the real, must be inscribed at the center of reflection on time and covenant. It does so in a way that honors the legitimate human search for understanding the structures of the real that, far from obscuring the meaning of history, provide the criteria for reflecting on it and living it. This is true for theology as well as for revelation. The latter is not exhausted by the prophetic books that stake out the route between creation and the final coming of Christ. It also consists of the Wisdom literature that treats in its own way physical realities, the nature of good and evil, morality, the nature of eternity, and being.

We can conclude with a calm admission of powerlessness. If it were possible to unite in one theory both relativity and quantum theory, then according to certain thinkers, we would have *the* formula for what is real. Likewise, if we could succeed at synthesizing Plato and Aristotle, we would have *the* philosophy, as the neo-Platonists at the beginning of the Christian era or those of the Renaissance tried to do. If we ignored the whole history of Western philosophy and returned directly to the pre-Socratic philosophers, and if we just succeeded in intellectually reconciling Parmenides and Heraclitus, we would arrive at *the* truth! In the same way, if we could be content with a single theological discourse that addressed the paschal mystery and the Incarnation, as well as the God of the Trinity and God's unity, the human being in his or her becoming and essence, we would have *the* theology. But then we would be God! In reality, the human spirit cannot in any domain arrive at discourse that is both true and exclusively one. We must resist the temptation to ignore one language in order to develop another exclusively. We cannot pit history against "being" or vice versa. There is wisdom in sailing by dead-reckoning between perspectives that are both true and difficult to reconcile and that we can discern in the Bible, in tradition, and in philosophy. In our day and our modern space, what I have proposed in this book is that the point of view we need to pay attention to, but not exclusively, should be that of history, but also that we cannot do so in some decisive and essential matters without the encounter with "being."

CONCLUSION
Open to the Future

At the beginning of the book, I wrote about salvation, meaning, and happiness. In the final analysis, these words express what all human beings search for and that are found only after much effort. Our deceptions, confusions, and frustrations in the face of constantly recurring evil create in us a sense of guilt and resentment. We feel guilt if the evil is attributed to failure, our own or someone else's, and resentment if it is due to factors beyond our control—a form of fatalism. This is seen also in our Western culture, which, having often taken leave of God, spares no one and is always trying to identify the culprits, even for natural disasters that supposedly society, the state, or the international community should have seen coming and should have taken preventive measures to avoid. Such hypersensitivity in matters of conscience and responsibility is curiously linked to a crushing sense of powerlessness. How can we explain the fact that unhappiness is so widespread? Is it possible for the elements to be less hostile and persons less violent? What can we say in the face of the finality of death, and is there anything beyond death? And, if the excess of evil outstrips all possible culpability, how can we deal with the sense of inevitability? Finally, in the midst of all this misery, how can we situate the human drive to know and to love, as well as our yearning for interior and external peace that nothing has been able to quench and that continues to search for appropriate human practices and expressions?

All religions and all forms of wisdom in the world have always strived to respond to such questions and to determine the actions that are most likely to improve the human condition. Formerly, but again today from time to time, we have imagined that there were extra-terrestrial beings whom we had offended by our actions and who needed to be appeased by onerous practices on our part that would have some effect on them, even though they are hard to identify. Didn't the primitive sin originate in the simple fact that human beings exist, and wasn't "creation" itself the primordial evil? Or again: who knows in the end? Maybe there is no god, or maybe Everything is god? How can we know what we must do? What mediators, geniuses, heroes, angels, idols, or stars can guide us in our profound ignorance? In looking at the world all around us and the world within us, we are tempted to say that, regarding all these questions, we are no more advanced in dealing with them than our ancestors, and that the painful enigma of unhappiness and happiness returns without interruption and unchanged.

In the midst of these more or less obscure quests and practices where moral and ritual elements were intertwined, Hellenism, Judaism, and then Christianity gradually emerged in our Western world. There are Athens and Jerusalem. In all its possible forms, the Greeks believed in *logos*. There is reason, and the absurd is not an option. Language must be true. The regular revolutions in the cosmos are eternal, and the rhythms on earth correspond to them. There is science. There is an art of living for men and women that corresponds to the *logos*. Coming from Plato's Academy, or Aristotle's Lyceum, or the Stoics' Porticoes ethics strives to establish this art by discovering the laws that define a practical human *logos*, the virtues that are in conformity with it, and the political structure that can best give it expression. Evil is found in disorder, from which it emerges and shows itself in many guises. As for death, either it enters by means of the rhythms of the cosmos, in which case we must accept it, even our own, or it marks disorder in the material world, and then the response must be to flee it. True *logos* is in the world that is Invisible. One might rejoin it by means of a spiritual adventure of purification (*catharsis*) and intellectual union (*gnosis*). As for speech regarding god or the gods, it has many forms and is uncertain. Is god the immanence of the *Logos* in the real? Is god the "Unknown god" beyond-everything-that-is? Salvation in any event would also be as "logical" as possible: by developing forms of contemplation that train one for the beyond; by remaining steadfast in a dignified human practice; by knowing how to enjoy riches, however limited, in the present moment; and by searching not for a happiness that would be superhuman, but by welcoming that which is within one's grasp.

Judaism and Christianity are different. They begin with God whose name is uttered from the beginning and is known progressively throughout the history that the people live with their God. Obscure divinities recede. A law of prayer and love takes shape, is perfected, and replaces the fanciful imagery of paganism. A sense of waiting takes form. Not the priests, the jurists, the sorcerers, or even the spirits and heroes gather the people but a "Son of Man" (see Daniel 7:13-14). Little by little his mission extends to the whole of humanity, leading them to God. There is the presentiment of a kingly reign, that is, a universal space where God will be confessed as Father and men and women will treat each other as brothers and sisters. Evil eludes the bonds of an undefined culpability or an obscure sense of inevitability, and is now attributed to true freedom. There is a vision, too, of universal forgiveness, the only means that can reveal the nature of human failure and can open the ways that lead to healing and that proceed from love.

Jesus Christ accomplishes and recapitulates in himself this long process. The final revealer of the name of God, he sums up, deepens, and interiorizes the law and the cult in reducing them to the commandment of love—of God, others, and oneself. He gathers a community that bears his mark, while always remaining provisional and open to everyone. He reveals and gives pardon, and he accomplishes the only authentic purification, the gift of his life by love. Risen from the dead, he will return. Cherished happiness is in waiting for this assured coming of the Risen One, and in the present moment is experienced in a life of interiority and mutual love. This vision of happiness does not exclude the history of evil and of suffering, since it imparts new power to confront them. This is the happiness of the Beatitudes.

Toward a World in the Form of Christendom

Just as it took a long time for the earth to be prepared to welcome Christ, so much time is needed (and we are a long way from having reached the goal) in order to recognize him as he is and to enter into the salvation he offers. First, there are the extremes of revelation that have been accented the most. Jesus is found both in the realm of the divine and in human misery. He is truly Son of God and Son of man in a world that is in a sorry state and in a humanity that is wounded. He is the one who satisfies our ultimate longing and wipes away our guilt. The effort to understand the factors involved in Christ's mediation has yielded impressive results. We have arrived at a mysterious awareness of God who puts our imaginary protagonists back to back: on the one side there are a multitude of gods created by us to relieve our fears, while on the other, something we might call the "Absolutely One." It is beyond or in the depths of everything that is, and the "Absolutely One" excludes all multiplicity. Whichever the case, such a god is pointless, since it has no relationship with human beings, or it is almighty and guarantees every totalitarian regime. The God of revelation, too, is One, but in his bosom he knows relationship and love, and the world he created is ordered to these very realities. Little by little, an awareness of human beings was attained, one in which human misery recedes and true humanity emerges. It is not a matter of covering up misery, but of coming to an awareness of mercy that not only forgives sinners but restores creatures to their world and gives them a new sense of openness and possibility. In order to understand the dimensions of this restoration of human beings in the truth, Hellenism made an immense contribution in making available the resources of its difficult but entirely honest anthropology.

This unheard-of disclosure of a new truth, both from God and from humanity, entailed many dangers. The facility with logic of the Christian of Greek culture constantly exposed him or her to the danger of forgetting the revealed character of such liberating knowledge and its inseparable bond with the church's historical witness. There was always a pronounced danger of changing the *witness* to Jesus Christ dead and risen into a coherent and obligatory *doctrine* with the threat of the loss of salvation. There was also the danger of ignoring what could be called the feeling of temporal and spatial fatigue in the progressive disclosure of knowledge of God, of Christ, and of the human being. Truth and error, good and evil, became absolute coordinates that no longer recognized the necessary conditioning of our statements and did not tolerate the hesitation that is inherent in human judgment and action. If, as experience showed, the disclosure of the truth did not eradicate the intractability and even the growth of evil, there was always the risk of a sense of bad conscience and a fear of damnation supplanting the blessed contemplation of human and divine splendor revealed in the Incarnation. The detailed prescriptions of the law risked robbing the joy of the ever new variability of the Holy Spirit. Such dangers, though, were not fatal, for there was never a lack of saintly men and women who showed in their lives the truth of salvation, the revelation of the face of God, and the appearance of humanity in Christ, along with the hope that sprang from them.

At the end of the patristic and medieval periods, perhaps one model gathered up the positive and negative aspects of the understanding of salvation as this long era came to a close. The Western church would willingly come to envision itself under the sign of a unified *Christendom*.

Confessing the same faith, administering the same sacraments, and obeying one Decalogue kept Christians united. The hierarchical structure of society, culminating in one government by the Roman Pontiff, would organize all Christians on the religious and the social planes. However different they were in the variety of their organization, the medieval theological *summae* offered the necessary global interpretations of the faith. A reunited humankind would be in a state of readiness as it awaited the coming of Christ, who would not delay much longer. Such a view did not lack its grandeur or, at the time, its effectiveness in spreading the gospel. It did, however, leave out the vast masses of humanity who had cut themselves off and were thereby judged to be culpable: heretics, Greek schismatics, Jews and Muslims, the supporters of the emperor or other political forces, without even counting those who sinned against God's law and the law of the church. It was also contested explicitly or implicitly within the church by spiritual movements that refused to recognize Christianity in a form that saw itself as the very apogee of Christian faith and practice. These movements were divided into two completely incompatible groups. First, there were those who were open to the development of human autonomy both personally and collectively in associations. According to them, salvation had to pass by way of a greater freedom, since Christ came precisely to rescue humanity from all forms of enslavement. In this perspective, an organization that was too massive would extinguish this freedom and human initiative. Then there were the poverty movements, some of which were balanced, while others exaggerated poverty. These did not envisage ultimate salvation as the passage of an organic Christendom journeying toward the kingdom of heaven, but as Christ's fearsome judgment coming to confound the arrogance and the wealth of this world, a judgment that only the poor, those faithful to the gospel, would be able to survive. All of this took concrete form in the person of St. Francis, in his gentleness and his unsurpassed power as the prophet sent by God before the end-time.

Toward a World in the Form of Globalization

With the arrival of what is called modernity, men and women claimed the right to discover their humanity, or in other words, the right to lead their lives in full freedom. But two interpretations of freedom soon took shape. The first affirms that in exercising freedom, not only does an individual not offend a god who is jealous of his own autonomy and authority, but the image of God is developed in us human beings. In mastering one's actions and one's destination, according to St. Thomas, humans imitate the all-powerful and wise God. Thomas' interpretation contains two elements: real autonomy of power and the inherent inscribing in us of our possibilities and our destiny, and being free, but in a human way (not in a divine or angelic way). For humans to be free includes several ideas. It is to be invited to the "knowledge" of God, not to an impossible voluntary self-transformation. It means to be confronted in love, the only commandment, by others who are also images of God, whose humanity is common to our own, but also in their singularity. And it is the possibility of dialogue, since it is a matter of two original freedoms existing in a common space for humanity.

The second interpretation, which can be identified emblematically with William of Ockham, totally rejects any inherent limitation on freedom and places no value on the notion of the image of God, even though it is not ignorant of the theme. The human being is alone in his or her singularity and power to act. It is less a matter of the Image of God channeling our freedom, than the might of God (which we really cannot truly conceptualize) limiting our own power, a might we always have to reckon with. God is the more powerful vis-à-vis humans. As for humans vis-à-vis one another, equipped with an absolute singularity, the situation is entirely different, because there is nothing common that unites men and women. Here, too, the conflict of powers is ever present, since there is nothing objective one can rely on to direct a discussion or to reach a compromise. The understanding of evil is also changed. Human beings in the classical approach are always "other," and so can offend God and other men and women by the hubris of their will. That usually happens when, in a given situation, they neglect to define the conduct that is in accord with human nature and corresponds to their singular vocation. One might have to ask for forgiveness, but also to try to correct the evil, in the measure one can do so, so that both parties can progress on the true trajectory of freedom. Modern human beings are confronted by pure conflict, because there is no intelligible norm governing their actions. For them, law can only constrain them and the way appears to be free for the return of fatalism, if we mean by this word the inevitable clash of rival powers, a world of violence always already there. I said that Ockham was emblematic of this understanding of human nature, but I could just as easily have said Thomas Hobbes (1588–1679). In a real sense, Hobbes is the true descendent of Ockham.

Must we, then, take leave of the modern human being, ceaselessly poised between a freedom without boundaries or direction and the growing oppression of evil? Are we only capable of fashioning an ethics and defining a political structure that pits men and women against each other in endless wars, grounded on growing injustices? We cannot entertain the dream of returning to the days of Christendom, but must we simply return to the classical view of the human being elaborated in the morality and the politics of a St. Thomas Aquinas and nourished, in what pertains to the faith at least, by the cautious equilibrium worked out by the Council of Trent?

The hypothesis I have developed in this short book, and that I have argued in other writings of mine, is that the modern human being has discovered something that the classical understanding, even that of St. Thomas, did not have occasion to learn, namely, that in the encounter of freedoms, God's and the human being's, or that of human beings with each other, there is a moment of conflict that is unavoidable and beneficial. The particularity of a freedom totally preoccupied with the infinity of its own desires clashes with that of another particular freedom that is just as ambitious. The resolution of the conflict forces a person to surpass his or her will, in order to make room for the other's desire, and vice versa. And so, together, both freedoms find themselves in a new space, reduced in so far as the first ambition that each had, but enlarged by the interrelationship and the extent of the other's claim. The Bible speaks in this way from beginning to end, but a great deal of time was needed for us to understand the message.

And so, it follows that the ultimate positive motive of history is love, in the active sense of the word, that is, to give one's own life, so that the other might be, and if we ourselves want to be, then we must receive life from the other. Whoever loses his or her life gains it. With that insight, the view of the human being of classical anthropology and the Council of Trent is not lost, since the mutual giving cannot succeed without the values they advocate, namely, reflecting on and discerning the measure to which the gift is realized in truth. The tragic misfortune is that this exchange of freedoms that is constitutive of humanity throughout history, does not happen at all or happens poorly, and that the slightest failure in communication has repercussions on inter-human relations, as well as relations with the world, and finally with God. The formidable structures of sin are mobilized. Salvation, then, is revealed in the appearance of the love of God as God is, that is, Father, Son, and Holy Spirit. Here, the self-giving is constant and the joy perfect, since everything is given unendingly. This love is shown in the paschal mystery of Jesus Christ that gives incarnate form on earth to the eternal movement of the Son. It is actively manifested by the gift of the Holy Spirit who helps us come to know God in us by learning to die for each other.

Might we now risk several proposals regarding the global form the world is assuming today? The classical period came to an end with its dream of a united Christendom. At the present moment of the period of modernity, humanity sees itself under the sign of globalization. However, the concept does not date from today, and in the recent past efforts were made to assure a measure of political stability, as with the "League of Nations" and then the "United Nations." Globalization assumes greater proportions today, where it appears both unavoidable and dangerous. It is unavoidable because history accelerates in a way that always negates time and space. The means of communication are such today that there is virtually no delay between an event and its being broadcast on the news, between an economic transaction and its immediate effect, and between political decisions being made and the effect those decisions will have on entire populations. It is dangerous because such rapidity of exchange tends to ignore persons, groups, and cultures—everything that needs time and space to ripen, to find its place, to develop harmoniously, and to maintain relationships. Globalization might be the final fruit of triumphant modernity, founded on liberalism, the *mos mathematicum* I've spoken about, and the radical forgetfulness of the human. This fruit would only result in an increasingly smaller class of masters, deploying their worldwide influence on those at the bottom of an ever-growing impoverishment of the greater mass of men and women.

Just as in the Middles Ages it was the poor who rose up in the face of a Christendom they judged to be monolithic, so today it is the poor who rise up in opposition to a globalization that they judge to be crushing them. In order to avoid the danger that my reference to the poor will be thought romantic and unreal, I need to further specify what I mean by the "poor." I ask myself whether the phrase "the poor" should not be identical with "human beings." In essence, it would express the following: their desires, their rights, and their duties, that is, their freedom in the face of God, others, and themselves. In other words, the human being "is only man, nothing more," to quote St. Francis de Sales once again.

If we look to the poor's earthbound existence, it is characterized by destitution, and if we look to their higher nature, it demands that no human being should be deprived of a poverty that is constitutive of who they are. In other words, the norm of development is the other and others, so that all together can be human. This is the point of being human that requires dialogue, but dialogue based on love, or the capacity to lose one's life in order to gain it, that is, what above I have called tragedy. This word "tragedy" also means what might be referred to as the second level of poverty. Even the initial ensemble of desires, rights, and duties must succumb to disequilibrium, so that it can play its role in a dialectic of gift. A person gives what he or she has and receives what is offered in return. Here we find ourselves at the very root of how different groups of human beings are formed and sustain themselves. The other and others are not beings-in-general; they differentiate and organize themselves in accordance with their sexuality, their history, and their cultures, so that on these collective levels, exchange can occur. This is the point at which, furthermore, the role of the mediation of reason and in a sense of "nature," too, is unavoidable. Reason facilitates effective exchange as a real possibility and not just a romantic dream.

Experience shows that keeping these two levels of poverty—the minimum a person needs to exist and the many forms of human exchange—presupposes prolonged struggle in order to reject tragedy in its other sense, the "tragic misfortune" of inequalities, and to eradicate the always actual structures of sin bound up with the history of the unwarranted appropriation of others' rights and goods, so that every poor human being might be able to triumph over it. This is the form of human misery that in Latin America is called being a "non-person." It has become a reference point that indicates situations in which it is not enough simply to come to the assistance of the poor by providing for their material needs, but one must also be open to the possibility of their responsibly engaging in the essence of human exchange and so becoming a "poor person" and no longer a "non-person." In all honesty, we need to ask if truly authentic globalization will ever be possible. We would have to establish an economics, a politics, an anthropology, and a theology *that starts with human misery and takes into consideration the situation of the poor and in a way that takes these words with utter seriousness.* How can humanity, left to its own devices and in the midst of a confused and sinful history, redress the situation, that is, how can humanity reestablish rectitude in a situation that is historically profoundly distorted?

In such a situation, we can understand that the powerful currents of Christian thought must place greater weight today not only on Christ's poverty but on the sense of destitution Christ was subjected to. If he took the last place, it was because it defines what it is to be human at the fundamental level (what I called the level of desire, rights, and duties), and then at the level of his suffering humiliation as a person deprived even of essentials. There, at that level, Jesus faced the Other, God his Father, who offered the covenant in his word. Jesus risked his life in God's covenant that led him to become the servant of all men and women by assuming his role, at his point in history, in the tragic misfortune of division and bringing the human situation to completion by dying. To die for men and women, and so reorient them to the gift, implies restoring the dignity they had at the beginning.

Perhaps globalization, like Christendom in former times, is the projection of hope of the kingdom of heaven—a hope that is more or less explicitly sensed by Christians at this historical moment. That is why we do not perceive it here below, at least not as the end-effect of our efforts. Nevertheless it will come, but through the intervention of those men and women who, by remaining uncompromisingly faithful to their religion and their convictions, will have sacrificed themselves by their human engagement on behalf of the dignity of the poor and who, when all is said and done, will have died for them. These men and women will be those who have "watched with Christ in Gethsemani" (Dietrich Bonhoeffer), and did not fall asleep so long as Christ is in agony up to the end of the world (Blaise Pascal [1623–1662]), and at the same time have acted for their fellow men and women with reflection, measured action, and risk. Those who will have tried to "come to help on God's behalf" and who have been overtaken by human malice, will have suffered for others while all the time being able to admire the beauty of creation and the intrinsic goodness of humanity, over and above their perversities (Etty Hillesum [1914–1943]).[1] But also those who have believed in the possibility of love's triumph over hatred and of effecting improbable reconciliations on the level of politics (Robert Schuman [1886–1963] and Edmond Michelet [1899–1970]), or of religion and who have in the end given their lives (Mohandas Gandhi [1869–1948], Martin Luther King, Jr. [1929–1968], Bishop Oscar A. Romero [1917–1980], the seven Trappist monks of the Monastery of Tibhirine, Algeria, murdered in May 1996,[2] Pierre Claverie, bishop of Oran, Algeria, murdered in August 1996). The few names I have been able to recall in this context (and I could add so many more of persons known or anonymous), are so many icons that appear at the conclusion of our "theological journey." They bring our pilgrimage to a close and point to those men and women under whose auspices we must continue the demanding work of Christian reflection.

---

[1] See Etty Hillesum, *An Interrupted Life* (New York: Pantheon, 1983) [translator].
[2] See John W. Kiser, *The Monks of Tibhirine: Faith, Love, and Terror in Algeria* (New York: St. Martin's Press, 2002) [translator].

APPENDIX ONE
A Glossary of Terms

Prepared by John J. Burkhard, O.F.M. Conv.

Usually, Ghislain Lafont provides an explanation of some of the basic terms he treats in his book, but not always. I have appended this "glossary" in the form of very short essays to help the general reader better understand the author's work. What follows are my explanations of a number of general theological ideas.

Apocalypse/Apocalyptic

An apocalypse or apocalyptic thought is a later form of prophetic speech in Judaism. It arose in times of stress or persecution of the Jews. As such, it developed to a high degree the ability to speak about Judaism's stressful existence without naming the persecutor directly, but pointing in that direction by signs and images appropriate to the situation. These signs and images are often very graphic, fanciful, lurid, and terrifying. The intent was not to frighten readers, but to encourage them to continued resistance or perseverance in the face of often heightened persecution. Apocalyptic literature, then, is resistance literature that intends to encourage and offer hope. It is not to be taken literally as predicting Israel's future or specific actions by God, so much as helping Israel cope with oppression in the present. This genre was also adopted by Christian writers when they, too, faced persecution by religious or secular authorities who opposed nascent Christianity, e.g., the book of Revelation. Apocalyptic also helped introduce newer ideas related to Christianity, e.g., the resurrection of the dead and final judgment, ideas that were not to be found clearly stated in the other scriptural forms of expression—the law, the prophets, Israel's histories, and the wisdom writings.

Economy of salvation

In a theological context, "economy" means an order or stage of affairs. We can speak of "economy" as relating human, as well as divine, realities. In antiquity, "economy" pointed to a whole that helped one understand and situate the parts. The economy of salvation became a way of speaking about how God acted in the history of Israel to enter into covenant with Israel and to preserve this covenant in the face of external opposition by her enemies or by her own sinful actions. With the life, death, and resurrection of Jesus, Christians interpreted their existence in terms of what the Lord had done for them in redeeming them and in giving them a way of life by his teachings and his lifestyle. The divine economy refers to that order or realm that seeks to express God's very life and plan, and comes close to what Western thinkers call God's immanence or presence to creatures.

End-time

This technical term refers to the events associated with the consummation of God's plan for creation, and for humankind in particular, that will be accomplished by Christ as Lord of creation and of history. The phrase "end-time" or "end-times" points to the ultimate hopes of the church and includes such events as the return of Jesus in glory, the last judgment, and the end of the world. Contemporary Scripture scholars and theologians explain it somewhat differently than former generations of believers and scholars. Today, the end-time and its attendant events are regarded more positively and integrally. These events are understood as expressions of the fullness of human salvation, and the fate of humankind is not isolated from that of the whole universe, which is also God's creation. The fear-inspiring events of the end-time are often derived from apocalyptic thought forms (see "Apocalypse/Apocalyptic"). Today, however, theologians are inclined to explain these trials in terms of how they can be seen as helping Christians grow and mature in their faith. Their primary intention is not to show God's will to punish creatures. Other dimensions of the church's teaching concerning the end-time include complete human beatitude (heaven), the possibility of damnation (hell), and an experience of coming to full human and spiritual integration (dying and death, and for Roman Catholics, some form of a doctrine of purgatory). However it is understood, the Christian doctrine of an end-time is meant to inspire hope in God's ultimate purposes, not fear.

Eschatology/Eschatological

Judaism was powerfully influenced by the goodness of creation, the utter gratuitousness of the covenant, and the sinfulness of Israel as God's covenant partner. This state of affairs meant that there was always a disparity between God's intentions and Israel's response. An eschatological view of God's purposes foresaw a time or a situation when God's plans would be realized perfectly. This time or situation would be God's last or final act on behalf of Israel. How God would accomplish this "eschatological act" was the subject of much speculation—directly or indirectly through the agency of a Messiah or a Son of Man or Adam Perfected or some other such figure—but the act itself always remained a lively hope of Israel. It implied such themes as peace, security, well-being in all its dimensions, and an undreamt-of presence of God to Israel. It was fostered by language and images of fulfillment and contentment: the perfect marriage of husband and wife, a banquet, a fig tree or vineyard, and a peaceful kingdom. Eventually, it came to express the hopes of some in Israel that their Covenant God intended the universal happiness of humankind and not just Israel's fulfillment. See also "Realized eschatology/Future eschatology."

Expiation

The New Testament is abundantly clear in declaring that men and women are saved by Jesus through his death and resurrection. Nonetheless, the Bible employs a whole range of ideas and images in spelling out the nature of this act of being saved. Expiation is one of those ideas. It derives from Christians claiming that expiation was accomplished in Jesus' sacrifice on the cross and in the shedding of his blood. In the Judaism that was the soil of Christian theology, expiation took place primarily on the Day of Atonement, Yom Kippur, and was accomplished by the high priest in the Temple in Jerusalem. As an image, then, expiation is an expression of a specific cultic act that took place in the Temple. In the minds of some early Christians, the annual cult-act of atonement was replaced by Christ's violent death on the cross. Christ's blood, then, expiated or "purified in blood" humankind of their sins. Guilt, blood, and cultic activity are all wrapped up in the idea of expiation. The danger with the image is in isolating and exaggerating the feature of blood. The advantage is found in making sense out of Jesus' tragic and undeserved crucifixion—a "curse" according to Galatians 3:13. Like the other ideas and images for salvation—deliverance, ransom, liberation, reconciliation, and justification—expiation stands in need of being complemented by them.

Gospel

Before there were the written gospels, there was the oral proclamation of the good news by Jesus, and then by the early church. Jesus proclaimed the Gospel of the kingly rule of God (see Kingdom of God below), while the early church proclaimed the Gospel of Jesus' life, death, and resurrection, together with the meaning of these God-directed and God-vindicated acts. In this broader sense, the Gospel is more than a message or defined contents, it is a power to save. Already in proclaiming his Gospel, Jesus was offering salvation to his hearers. Already in proclaiming their Gospel, Peter, Paul, and the other apostles were inviting their hearers to salvation here and now. The Gospel calls persons to faith in Jesus Christ and to the believer's commitment to Jesus' "way" or lifestyle. The Gospel is characterized by love of God and one's fellow human beings (neighbors and enemies) according to Mark 12:29-31; to mercy, forgiveness and reconciliation; to acts of justice; to the ways of peace; to poverty as detachment and generosity; and to the acceptance of persecution when it comes one's way. The heart of the Gospel way of discipleship is spelled out in the Beatitudes recorded in Matthew 5:3-12 and Luke 6:20-23.

Grace

Grace is not some "thing." It is a dimension of the mystery of God as Trinity. The Second Letter of Peter is the foundational text for understanding grace: "that you may come to share in the divine nature" (1:4). Contemporary theologians have returned to the priority of stressing grace as the self-communication of God to men and women, sometimes called "uncreated grace." In an effort to preserve God's transcendence in the face of human choices and sinfulness, and given the absolutely gratuitous character of grace, some theologians stressed grace as a created gift that enables individuals to share in the divine life and to live out that life. This had two unfortunate consequences: grace came to be understood primarily as an aid in living the Christian life envisioned as a moral and spiritual struggle, and grace was seen to be something quantifiable—one had "more" or "less" grace, one was *in* "the state of grace" or one had fallen *out of* it. Today, the stress is on relational terms that are seen as more appropriate to personhood, divine and human. Grace is our human sharing in the Trinity's very life and the relationships that flow from the life of the trinitarian persons. There is still a place for "actual graces" from God, but they are always grounded in the prior grace that elevates the creature to the divine life.

Kingdom of God

In Mark we read, "After John had been arrested, Jesus came to Galilee, proclaiming the gospel of God: 'This is the time of fulfillment. The kingdom of God is at hand'" (1:14-15). Jesus' ministry, then, was centered on proclaiming the kingdom of God or God's kingly rule. Both translations are used by scholars. The first stresses its concreteness, the second its active power. The first lends itself to a more static interpretation, while the second is more dynamic. Scholars debate whether this rule is an idea or concept, or a symbolic representation. The contents of this kingly rule are hard to summarize, since the kingdom contains unrealized elements and the time frame for the kingdom keeps shifting—now at hand, now present, now future. Scholars speak of the temporality of the kingdom as "already" and "not yet" to state this blurring of a chronological perspective. God's kingly rule is clearly a matter of hope as much as a matter of possession. A more symbolic reading of the kingdom of God aims at uniting these disparate yet complementary elements while preserving their inherent tension. The prophets before Jesus used just such symbols and symbolic actions in their efforts to call Israel to full covenant life with God. The kingdom of God, then, is a profound element of Jewish and Christian eschatology.

Mystery

The term "mystery" points to the unsearchable depths of reality. God is mystery par excellence, not because God is unknowable to human reason but because God is inexhaustibly knowable by humans. We live from mystery as that dimension of human existence that lures us more and more into richer life, truth, and power.

Mystery is not frustration at our not being able to master certain questions or dimensions of life, but endless enjoyment in its ever-deeper meaningfulness. The human experience of mystery opens us for understanding God as Divine Mystery. We delight in mystery because God as the Ground of Mystery invites us into its endless source. Mystery differs from a problem or a puzzle, since these are meant to be solved and in principle are open to humans resolving their questions, contradictions, and tensions. Our human sense of mystery and our being grasped by Divine Mystery open us up to deeper levels of understanding. Mystery questions the all-sufficiency of certain forms of rationality by opening us to other levels of knowing. These exaggeratedly rational forms can be based on scientific reductionism, human behaviorism, materialistic evolutionism, or Marxist materialism. But mystery also critiques such unworthy responses as radical skepticism, relativism, and religious superstition in the face of the vastness and obscurity of human knowledge. Mystery calls for surrender on our part, but a surrender that promises light, fulfillment, and greater meaning. In biblical language, Jesus Christ is the revelation of God's mysterious plan for humankind (see Eph 1:9).

Myth

Myth has contributed greatly to human and religious understanding. In fact, human beings need it; myth is an essential way humans create and express meaning. But the term "myth" is also the source of much confusion. Many feel that myth belongs to a primitive stage of knowing and to inexact knowledge. It is destined to be surpassed by the concepts of the exact sciences: physics and biology, history, sociology, and psychology. However, myth is concerned with establishing and maintaining identity and imparting meaning to humans. Explanation is secondary in the realm of myth. Societies and civilizations recount their myths in order to attend to who they are and how they are distinguished from other societies. Myth is not the opposite of factual knowledge, and so connotations of myth as fictitious or deliberately deceiving are not accurate. Myth operates on the human mind, emotions, and imagination in ways that seek to communicate truth where this truth is resistant to the simple summarization of facts, propositional statements, or the formulation of hypotheses. Myths operate with the resources of narratives told by societies, with ageless traditions, and with symbols and archetypes. Though they operate on the level of human consciousness, their real ground is the Unconscious, both personal and collective. Myths employ language, but highly imaginative, suggestive, and allusive vocabulary and symbols. See also "Symbol."

Original Sin

In a world where we are familiar with vast millennia of cosmic and human evolution, and where Adam and Eve can no longer be regarded as historical figures, the church's teaching on Original Sin will necessarily demand reformulation. Efforts to reformulate it, however, have yielded little consensus among theologians in the way that St. Augustine's teaching did for almost fifteen hundred years. Some theologians claim that Original Sin is a way of saying that men and women, who are naturally good, sin and thus corrupt their personal situations and their societies. Others maintain that Original Sin is the situation of sinfulness that all humans are born into, and thus, even though the infant does not commit personal sins, the infant, too, comes under the real power of sin. According to this interpretation, no human being is free from sin, except by personal privilege, e.g., the Mother of God. Contemporary theologians are searching for a middle position between these two. In theory, the real personal sins of humankind so affect us that we are positively predisposed to commit sin rather than to avoid it. Nevertheless, in God's plan for salvation, saving grace is available to each and every human being. Grace is always stronger than sin (see Rom 5:20), and the teaching of the Bible unquestionably gives the priority to grace. Just as we are in solidarity with "Adam" in sin, so are we in solidarity with Christ in being offered salvation. The doctrine of Original Sin reminds us of what is at stake for humanity, but from the negative pole of experience, or our failures, whereas grace reminds us of what is at stake from the positive pole of the experience of hope for salvation. The doctrine also serves as an antidote for the constant temptation to trivialize the destructiveness of sin and its tragic consequences. Original Sin is not the mere addition of all the personal sins of men and women throughout history. Rather, it both includes all these sins and views them as the context within which men and women necessarily exercise their own personal freedom—a situation of precariousness and of solidarity with the whole of humankind.

Plurality/Pluralism

Increasingly, plurality or diversity is a mark of human experience. The explosion of knowledge, the instant communication of information by the media and the Internet, and the shrinking of the world because of the modern means of travel offer a wide spectrum of facts, views, interpretations, and mind-sets to contemporary men and women. Even in religion, but within bounds, a variety of ideas and practices no longer pose the threat to a person's faith or world view as they did formerly. The documents of Vatican II and the post-conciliar papal magisterium even praise the benefits of plurality and acknowledge the fact that there has always been such diversity in the church. Thus, we can point to differences between Eastern and Western official theologies, differences in liturgical practice throughout the church (e.g., the Latin and the Eastern rites among Roman Catholics), and the innumerable spiritualities in the church. We even accept with equanimity the diversity of literary genres, ideas, perspectives, and theologies in the New Testament. All of this has created a new attitude in the church that in accepting diversity we can avoid the rigid uniformity of the recent past. More importantly, the acceptance of diversity creates the proper space for the fostering of personal freedom. Nevertheless, as diversity expands, so, too, does pluralism. Nevertheless, diversity always comes with conflict and some confusion over which idea is "best." Some claim that the positions of those who seek to know reality are so irreconcilable that we are left with a world where only individual choice can resolve the conflict of interpretations. Individual preference thus trumps any sense of objective or communally accepted truth or meaning. Pluralism in this radical form is sometimes called relativism, and clearly cannot be accepted by believers. However, with caution, some positive evaluation of pluralism is possible in a postmodern world.

Realized eschatology/Future eschatology

In attempting to reconcile the difference of time frame for the kingdom of God, scholars distinguish various forms of eschatology. Scholars like C. H. Dodd (1884–1973) were so impressed by the note of fulfillment in John's gospel that they opted for this "realized" form of eschatology as the most original. This interpretation saw Jesus' ministry, death, and resurrection as the announcement of the kingdom's arrival, but left little room for any future salvific events. Others preferred the "future" or unfulfilled interpretation, understanding Jesus' ministry as the real but still dawning initiation of the kingdom. This interpretation makes room for eschatological development in history and leaves open the possibility of humans contributing to the coming of God's kingdom in its fullness. It elicited human effort and led to such movements as the "social gospel," a church movement that focused on establishing the kingdom of God on earth now through service to the poor and moral reform. Still others preferred a middle position by maintaining that what Jesus preached was the kingdom in the state of always arriving. Jesus' agency was thus maintained and the statements in the Gospel could be held in tension but as having meaning—salvation is an ever present reality, yet one that is not to be presumed but always received as gift. Christians continue to await a final event that will bring the cosmos and human history to completion. Finally, there were a few like Albert Schweitzer (1875–1965) who claimed that Jesus indeed expected an "imminent" end during his lifetime that never happened. In this view, the early church was sadly mistaken in adopting Jesus' viewpoint. See also "Eschatology."

Sacrament

All Christians accept sacraments as gifts from Christ that have to do with grace. We differ, however, on their number and their importance. After the Council of Trent (1545–1563), a highly individualized sacramental theology took hold and teamed up with the stress on "created grace" or actual graces (see also "Grace") to stress the need for the frequent reception of certain sacraments, especially penance and the Eucharist. A mechanical sense of sacramental grace became a real danger. At Vatican II, the bishops tried to understand the relationship of the sacraments to life in the church and taught that "the church, in Christ, is in the nature of sacrament—a sign and instrument, that is, of communion with God and of the unity of the entire human race" (*Lumen Gentium* par. 1). The teaching that the sacraments are celebrated by and in the church helped reduce the risk of an overly individualized understanding of the sacraments and gave greater attention to the interpersonal dimensions of the sacraments. Thereby, the council reoriented Roman Catholic sacramental theology in a fundamental way. The Catholic tendency after Trent to separate the proclamation of the Word of God from sacramental activity was also mitigated in the revised sacramental rites after the council. Today, sacraments are understood as realizations of Christian discipleship that always takes place in the community, the church. The sacraments help bring about our continual conversion as we seek to conform to Christ. Every sacramental celebration is also the realization of the church, or the church-in-act. Salvation is fundamentally social in nature, and sacraments are celebrations of the community. Moreover, men and women are creatures who are bound to symbols for their self-understanding, self-realization, and relationships. Sacraments, then, participate in the nature of symbolic actions. Finally, sacraments are understood best when they are seen within a system of sacramental acts rather than isolated from one another as so many individual actions that affect limited dimensions of the recipient. Every sacrament is addressed to the whole person as a person in community.

Symbol

In the preceding entry, I said that humans are symbolic creatures. Symbols are one of the essential ways that we realize ourselves. In recent years, anthropologists, psychologists, linguistic scholars, literary critics, and philosophers have shown increased interest in symbols. They distinguish between "signs" that operate more on the surface and on the level of our consciousness, from "symbols" that are found in the Unconscious and at the deeper, not easily accessible levels of human consciousness. Symbols seem to be inscribed in the human psyche and its unconscious life. A symbol not only conveys meaning, it constitutes it. Some explain its power by claiming that a symbol, while remaining what it is in itself, also participates in another reality that it conveys. Think, for instance, of such primordial symbols as fire, water, birth, and death. They cannot be restricted to only one level of signification and meaning, since they operate on multiple levels. Others explain the power of symbols by claiming that they operate dialectically, i.e., by taking advantage of the oppositions and tensions inherent in complex realities. Instead of trying to eliminate the oppositions, symbols organize and work with them by allowing each to express some aspect of reality. Sacraments share certain characteristics of symbols. They are unitive, constituting wholeness in the person and among persons. They have an inexhaustible depth of meaning, and so nourish the human spirit. They introduce persons into deeper levels of presence and co-presence. Finally, and most especially, they communicate the divine life by means of the physical or human realities that are represented. In all of this, sacraments would seem to be special realizations of human symbolic activity and open to explanation, at least in part, by symbolic theory.

Trinity: Economic and Immanent

Theologians speak of the "economic Trinity" when they refer to God as Father, Son, and Spirit acting in the order or "economy" of salvation, i.e., in creation, in redeeming humankind from sin, and in bringing all of creation to fulfillment (see also "Economy of salvation"). They speak of the "immanent Trinity" when they refer to God as Father, Son, and Spirit sharing/acting/living within God's own life and not as shared with what is not God, i.e., creation. In the early church, the Trinity was spoken of in economic terms drawn directly from the scriptural sources—terms that spoke of how the Trinity related to us. Eventually, the pressures that arose from the human mind struggling with God's transcendence *and* God's presence to us caused a shift toward the use of speculative terms like "nature," "person," and "processions"—all characteristic of an immanent perspective. Little by little, the theology of God's own Trinitarian existence, lived and shared among the "Three Persons of the Blessed Trinity," overshadowed the equally valid, and in some sense the always normative (because biblical) economic perspective. The theology of the "immanent Trinity" showed an excessive preoccupation with the question of how the triune God could be one and three at the same time, and whether priority was to be shown to the "oneness" or the "threefoldness." One needs to avoid driving a wedge between these two ways of understanding and proclaiming Trinitarian belief. The Trinity can be perceived as economic and immanent in different contexts without contradiction.

APPENDIX TWO
Writings in English by
and about Ghislain Lafont, O.S.B.

PREPARED BY JOHN J. BURKHARD, O.F.M. CONV.

Writings of Ghislain Lafont in English

"Analogy," "Language. I. Philosophical Language," and "Time and Temporality." In *Dictionary of Fundamental Theology*, edited by René Latourelle and Rino Fisichella, 5–7, 595–600, and 1113–1119. New York: Crossroad, 1995.

"The Eucharist in Monastic Life." *Cistercian Studies* 19 (1984) 296–318.

"Fraternal Correction in the Augustinian Community." *Word and Spirit* 9 (1987) 87–91.

God, Time, and Being. Translated by Leonard Maluf. Petersham, MA: Saint Bede's Publications, 1992 [1986].

Imagining the Catholic Church: Structured Communion in the Spirit. Translated by John J. Burkhard. Collegeville, MN: The Liturgical Press, 2000.

"Notes on the Spiritual Aspect of Fraternal Relations." *Cistercian Studies* 2/3 (1974) 221–25.

Articles in English on the Theology of Ghislain Lafont, O.S.B.

Blaylock, Joy Harrell. "Ghislain Lafont and Contemporary Sacramental Theology." *Theological Studies* 66 (2005) 841–61.

Driscoll, Jeremy, ed. *"Imaginer la théologie catholique,"* Permanence et transformations de la foi en attendant Jésus-Christ. Mélanges offerts à Ghislain Lafont. Rome: Pontificio Ateneo S. Anselmo, 2000.

———. "Liturgy and Fundamental Theology." *Ecclesia Orans* 11 (1994) 69–99, at 82–89.

————. "The Manifestation of the Trinitarian Mystery in the Eucharistic Assembly." In *"Imaginer la théologie catholique,"* edited by Jeremy Driscoll, 501–13.

Haight, Roger. "Towards an Ecclesiology from Below." In *"Imaginer la théologie catholique,"* edited by Jeremy Driscoll, 413–36, at 422–28.

Hunt, Anne. "Ghislain Lafont: Death and Being, Human and Divine." *The Trinity and the Paschal Mystery: A Development in Recent Catholic Theology.* Collegeville, MN: The Liturgical Press, 1997. 37–56.

APPENDIX THREE
Suggestions for Further Reading

PREPARED BY JOHN J. BURKHARD O.F.M. CONV.

Chapter One: The Scriptures

Armstrong, Karen. *A History of God: The 400-Year Quest of Judaism, Christianity and Islam.* New York: Alfred A. Knopf, 1993.

————. *The Great Transformation: The Beginning of Our Religious Traditions.* New York: Alfred A. Knopf, 2006.

Becker, Jürgen. *Paul, Apostle to the Gentiles.* Translated by O. C. Dean. Louisville, KY: Westminster John Knox Press, 1993.

Brown, Raymond E. *An Introduction to the New Testament.* New York: Doubleday, 1997.

————. *The Death of the Messiah: From Gethsemane to the Grave,* 2 vols. New York: Doubleday, 1994.

Brueggemann, Walter. *A Social Reading of the Old Testament: Prophetic Approaches to Israel's Communal Life.* Edited by Patrick D. Miller. Minneapolis: Fortress Press, 1994.

Dunn, James D. G. *The Theology of Paul the Apostle.* Grand Rapids, MI: Wm. B. Eerdmans, 1998.

Durrwell, François-Xavier. *The Resurrection: A Biblical Study.* Translated by Rosemary Sheed. New York: Sheed and Ward, 1960.

Jaspers, Karl. *The Origin and Goal of History.* Translated by Michael Bullock. New Haven, CT: Yale University Press, 1953.

Meier, John P. *A Marginal Jew: Rethinking the Historical Jesus,* 3 vols. New York: Doubleday, 1991–2001.

Wright, N. T. *The Resurrection of the Son of God.* Minneapolis: Fortress Press, 2003.

Chapter Two: The Period of the "Fathers" and the "Councils"

Behr, John. *The Formation of Christian Theology,* 2 vols. Crestwood, NY: St. Vladimir's Seminary Press, 2001–2004.

Brown, Peter. *Augustine of Hippo: A Biography.* Expanded ed., Berkeley: University of California Press, 2000.

Evans, G. R., ed. *The First Christian Theologians: An Introduction to Theology in the Early Church.* Oxford: Blackwell, 2004.

Kelly, J. N. D. *Early Christian Doctrines.* Rev. ed. San Francisco: HarperCollins, 1978.

Osborn, Eric. *The Emergence of Christian Theology.* New York: Cambridge University Press, 1993.

Stark, Rodney. *The Rise of Christianity: A Sociologist Reconsiders History.* Princeton, NJ: Princeton University Press, 1996.

Young, Frances M. *From Nicaea to Chalcedon: A Guide to the Literature and its Background.* London: SCM Press, 1983.

Chapter Three: The Middles Ages

Brown, Peter. *The Rise of Western Christendom: Triumph and Diversity, AD 200–1000.* 2nd ed. Oxford: Blackwell, 2003.

Burr, David. *The Spiritual Franciscans: From Protest to Persecution in the Century after Saint Francis.* University Park: Pennsylvania State University Press, 2001.

Chadwick, Henry. *East and West: The Masking of a Rift in the Church, from Apostolic Times to the Council of Florence.* New York: Oxford University Press, 2003.

Chenu, Marie-Dominique. *Nature, Man, and Society in the Twelfth Century: Essays on New Theological Perspectives in the Latin West.* Edited and Translated by Jerome Taylor and Lester K. Little. Chicago: University of Chicago Press, 1968.

———. *Aquinas and His Role in Theology.* Translated by Paul Philibert. Collegeville, MN: The Liturgical Press, 2002.

Cullen, Christopher M. *Bonaventure.* New York: Oxford University Press, 2006.

Davies, Brian. *The Thought of Thomas Aquinas.* Oxford: Clarendon Press, 1992.

Delio, Ilia. *Crucified Love: Bonaventure's Mysticism of the Crucified Christ.* Quincy, IL: Franciscan Press, 1998.

———. *Simply Bonaventure: An Introduction to His Life, Thought, and Writings.* Hyde Park, NY: New City Press, 2001.

Delumeau, Jean. *Sin and Fear: The Emergence of a Western Guilt Culture, 13th–18th Centuries.* Translated by Eric Nicholson. New York: St. Martin's Press, 1990.

Evans, G. R. *Philosophy and Theology in the Middle Ages.* New York: Routledge, 1993.

Lambert, Malcolm D. *Franciscan Poverty: The Doctrine of the Absolute Poverty of Christ and the Apostles in the Franciscan Order 1210–1323.* St. Bonaventure, NY: Franciscan Institute, 1998.

Le Goff, Jacques. *Saint Francis of Assisi.* Translated by Christine Rhone. New York: Routledge, 2004.

Torrell, Jean-Pierre. *Saint Thomas Aquinas,* 2 vols. Translated by Robert Royal. Washington, DC: Catholic University of America Press, 1996–2003.

Chapter Four: The Modern Period
The Reformation

Cameron, Euan. *The European Reformation.* Oxford: Clarendon Press, 1991.

Lindberg, Carter, ed. *The Reformation Theologians: An Introduction to Theology in the Early Modern Period.* Oxford: Blackwell, 2002.

MacCulloch, Diarmaid. *The Reformation: A History.* New York: Viking, 2003.

McGrath, Alister E. *Reformation Thought: An Introduction.* 2nd ed. Oxford: Blackwell, 1993.

Oberman, Heiko A. *The Harvest of Medieval Theology: Gabriel Biel and Late Medieval Nominalism.* Cambridge, MA: Harvard University Press, 1963.

Steinmetz, David C. *Luther in Context.* Bloomington: Indiana University Press, 1986.

Modern Times

Armstrong, Karen. *The Battle for God.* New York: Alfred A. Knopf, 2000.

Barth, Karl. *Protestant Theology in the Nineteenth Century: Its Background and History.* New edition. Grand Rapids, MI: Wm. B. Eerdmans, 2002.

Berkhof, Hendrikus. *Two Hundred Years of Theology: Report of a Personal Journey.* Translated by John Vriend. Grand Rapids, MI: Wm. B. Eerdmans, 1989.

Dupré, Louis. *The Enlightenment and the Intellectual Foundations of Modern Culture.* New Haven, CT: Yale University Press, 2004.

———. *Passage to Modernity: An Essay in the Hermeneutics of Nature and Culture.* New Haven, CT: Yale University Press, 1993.

Ford, David F., ed. *The Modern Theologians: An Introduction to Christian Theology since 1918.* 3rd ed. Oxford: Blackwell, 2005.

Lash, Nicholas. *A Matter of Hope: A Theologian's Reflections on the Thought of Karl Marx.* Notre Dame, IN: University of Notre Dame Press, 1981.

MacIntyre, Alasdair C. *Three Rival Versions of Moral Enquiry: Encyclopedia, Genealogy and Tradition.* Notre Dame, IN: University of Notre Dame Press, 1990.

O'Malley, John W. *Trent and All That: Renaming Catholicism in the Early Modern Era.* Cambridge, MA: Harvard University Press, 2000.

Schwartz, Hans. *Theology in a Global Context: The Last Two Hundred Years.* Grand Rapids, MI: Wm. B. Eerdmans, 2005.

Twentieth-Century Roman Catholic Theologians

Kehl, Medard and Werner Löser, eds. *The von Balthasar Reader*. Translated by Robert J. Daly and Fred Lawrence. New York: Crossroad, 1985.

Lonergan, Bernard J. F. *Method in Theology*. New York: Herder and Herder, 1972.

McCool, Gerald A., ed. *A Rahner Reader*. New York: Crossroad, 1989.

Rahner, Karl. *The Content of Faith: The Best of Karl Rahner's Theological Writings*. Edited by Karl Lehmann and Albert Raffelt. New York: Crossroad, 1993.

———. *The Practice of Faith: A Handbook of Contemporary Spirituality*. Edited by Karl Lehmann and Albert Raffelt. New York: Crossroad, 1984.

Schreiter, Robert J., ed. *The Schillebeeckx Reader*. New York: Crossroad, 1984.

Chapter Five: Time and Divine Covenant

von Balthasar, Hans Urs. *Explorations in Theology*, 4 vols. Translated by A. V. Littledale, Alexander Dru, Brian McNeil, and Edward T. Oakes. San Francisco: Ignatius Press, 1989–1995.

Benedict XVI. *God is Love (Deus caritas est)* (December 25, 2005). Boston: Pauline Books and Media, 2006.

Evans, C. Stephen, ed. *Exploring Kenotic Christology: The Self-Emptying of God*. New York: Oxford University Press, 2006.

Rahner, Karl. *Foundations of Christian Faith: An Introduction to the Idea of Christianity*. Translated by William V. Dych. New York: Seabury, 1978.

Ratzinger, Joseph. *Introduction to Christianity*. Translated by J. R. Foster. Rev. ed. San Francisco: Ignatius Press, 2000.

Chapter Six: Creation and Being

Clayton, Philip D. *God and Contemporary Science*. Grand Rapids, MI: Wm. B. Eerdmans, 1997.

Edwards, Denis. *Breath of Life: A Theology of the Creator Spirit*. Maryknoll, NY: Orbis, 2004.

Ford, David F. *Theology: A Very Short Introduction*. New York: Oxford University Press, 1999.

Haught, John F. *Is Nature Enough? Meaning and Truth in the Age of Science*. New York: Cambridge University Press, 2006.

———. *Science and Religion: From Conflict to Conversation*. New York: Paulist Press, 1995.

Polkinghorne, John. *Faith, Science and Understanding*. New Haven, CT: Yale University Press, 2000.

———, ed. *The Work of Love: Creation as Kenosis*. Grand Rapids, MI: Wm. B. Eerdmans, 2001.

Volf, Miroslav. *Exclusion and Embrace: A Theological Exploration of Identity, Otherness, and Reconciliation*. Nashville, TN: Abingdon Press, 1996.

Conclusion: Open to the Future

Moltmann, Jürgen. *Theology Today: Two Contributions toward Making Theology Present*. Translated by John Bowden. Philadelphia: Trinity Press International, 1988.

Polkinghorne, John. *The God of Hope and the End of the World*. New Haven, CT: Yale University Press, 2002.

Some Research Resources

Alberigo, Giuseppe and Joseph A. Komonchak, eds. *History of Vatican II*, 5 vols. Maryknoll, NY: Orbis, 1995–2006.

Beinert, Wolfgang and Francis Schüssler Fiorenza, eds. *Handbook of Catholic Theology*. New York: Crossroad, 1995.

Brown, Raymond E., Joseph A. Fitzmyer and Roland E. Murphy, eds. *The New Jerome Biblical Commentary*. Englewood Cliffs, NJ: Prentice Hall, 1990.

Congar, Yves M.-J. *A History of Theology*. Edited and translated by Hunter Guthrie. Garden City, NY: Doubleday, 1968.

Fiorenza, Francis Schüssler and John P. Galvin, eds. *Systematic Theology: Roman Catholic Perspectives*, 2 vols. Minneapolis: Fortress Press, 1991.

Komonchak, Joseph A., Mary Collins and Dermot A. Lane, eds. *The New Dictionary of Theology*. Wilmington, DE: Michael Glazier, 1987.

Musser, Donald W. and Joseph L. Price, eds. *A New Handbook of Christian Theologians*. Nashville, Tenn.: Abingdon Press, 1996.

———. *A New Handbook of Christian Theology*. Enlarged edition. Nashville, TN: Abingdon Press, 2003.

O'Collins, Gerald and Edward G. Farrugia. *A Concise Dictionary of Theology*. Rev. ed. New York: Paulist Press, 2000.

Tanner, Norman P., ed. *Decrees of the Ecumenical Councils*, 2 vols. Washington, DC: Georgetown University Press, 1990.

INDEX OF NAMES

INDEX OF SUBJECTS